Memoirs of
a Russian Lady

Memoirs of a Russian Lady

Drawings and Tales of Life Before the Revolution

MARIAMNA DAVYDOFF

Selected and edited by Olga Davydoff Dax

Harry N. Abrams, Inc., Publishers, New York

Photography by Jean Pierre Pavillard
Designed by Sue Ebrahim

Library of Congress Cataloging-in-Publication Data

Davydoff, Mariamna Adrianovna, 1871–1961.
   Memoirs of a Russian lady.

   1. Davydoff, Mariamna Adrianovna, 1871–1961.
2. Soviet Union—Biography. I. Dax, Olga Davydoff.
II. Title.
CT1218.D38A36   1986   947.08′092′4 [B]   86–3361
ISBN 0-8109-0839-5

Times Mirror Books

Printed and bound in Hong Kong

CONTENTS

PREFACE

IN THE AUTUMN of 1983 I was travelling in the United States and called on a distant cousin of mine, Elena Lvovna Vassiloff, who lives on Long Island. Like me, she was born Davydoff and descended from Vassily Lvovich Davydoff, who had been exiled to Siberia because of his role in the Decembrist plot of 1825, when young Russian nobles made an unsuccessful attempt to overthrow the Tsar. Vassily Lvovich was her great-grandfather and my great-great-grandfather. Elena Lvovna, or Aliona, as she is called (a phonetic translation, always a problem when rendering Russian into a Western language), told me that she had three albums that her mother, Mariamna Adrianovna Davydoff, had left her. When I saw the quality of these little works of art that Mariamna herself had painted over fifty years earlier and that had remained hidden ever since, I felt they should be published – and that is how the idea of the present book was born.

Mariamna Adrianovna, the author of this book, was born Lopukhin, an old Russian family whose origins can be traced back to the eleventh century and whose ancestor Eudoxia married Peter the Great. The Lopukhins had been extremely wealthy and owned vast estates in the Ukraine; but Mariamna's grandfather, a notorious spendthrift, squandered his share of the family fortune, as did his brother's only son, so that Mariamna's father and his close relatives found themselves almost destitute.

On her mother's side, Mariamna came from an old and illustrious family, several of whose members played important roles in Russian history. Her mother's father, Ivan Orlov, was a Cossack chief and an extremely wealthy landowner; but here again his only son depleted the family fortune and was even forced to sell the family seat, Matussov. Mariamna's parents decided to buy Matussov in order to keep it in the family. To do this they not only had to sell the small estate her mother had received as a dowry, but also had to borrow from the banks. This put them in debt for the rest of their lives, and as the huge house and estate required a large staff and was very expensive to run they were forced to live in strict seclusion.

Mariamna was the second of five daughters, one of whom died in the 1890s. To recover from this sad event the family left Matussov for the first time and travelled to Paris, where Mariamna studied painting at the Académie Julian.

7

In 1899 Mariamna married Lev Alexeyevich Davydoff, a grandson of the Decembrist Vassily Lvovich, whose wife, Alexandra Ivanovna, was one of eleven heroic women that followed their husbands into exile. This couple had thirteen children, six born before the exile and seven after. Of the six, four were born before Vassily and Alexandra were married; Vassily's mother had opposed the match, and it was only after her death in January 1825 that they were able to marry. They had two sons before Vassily was sent to Siberia: Pyotr Vassilyevich, born in 1825, who married the daughter of another Decembrist, Prince Sergey Petrovich Trubetskoy (they were my great-grandparents), and Nicholas Vassilyevich, born in 1826, who never married. After Vassily Lvovich's condemnation these two became the sole legitimate heirs of the family estates which Vassily had inherited and from which he was deprived along with his rights and privileges.

The most important of these estates was the vast domain of Kamenka, which had been inherited through Prince Grigory Alexandrovich Potemkin, the well-known favourite of Catherine the Great. The nucleus of the estate was situated next to the village of Kamenka about 250 km south of Kiev. It comprised hundreds of thousands of hectares and included three large farming enterprises, Podlesnoe, Pliakovsky and Nikolaevsky, as well as many smaller estates where various members of the family settled and which became independent.

After leaving the army, the bachelor Nicholas Vassilyevich settled down in Kamenka and devoted his life to restoring it to its old status, whereas Pyotr went to live on his wife's estate in the Crimea. Nicholas never left Kamenka. He lived there with two of his unmarried sisters, Elisaveta ("Aunt Lisa"), born in 1823 before her parents' marriage, and Alexandra ("Aunt Sasha"), born in 1831 in Siberia.

One of the sons born in Siberia was Alexis Vassilyevich, the father of Mariamna's husband. Another one, Lev Vassilyevich, took over the management of the Kamenka estate, thus enabling Nicholas to devote his time to the study of philosophical, social and economic subjects. Lev Vassilyevich married Alexandra Ilyinishna, the sister of the composer Pyotr Ilyich Tchaikovsky, and they settled in Verbovka, a few kilometres from the village of Kamenka. Of their seven children, Yuri became the curator of the Tchaikovsky Museum in Klin where he died in 1965 (to be succeeded by his daughter Ksenya), and Dimitry ("Mitya") took over the Verbovka estate.

Another section of the Kamenka domain, known as Yurchikha, was given by Pyotr Vassilyevich to his only son, Vassily, my grandfather, who died in 1900. His widow, born Princess Olga Lieven, lived there with her three sons, the youngest of whom, Alexander Vassilyevich, was my father.

"Uncle Nicholas", who appears so often in Mariamna's paintings, lived in Kamenka in what was known as the Green House. It still exists and has become a museum called the Pushkin and Tchaikovsky Museum because of the frequent and prolonged visits that these two illustrious men made to Kamenka. Aunt Lisa and Aunt Sasha lived in the "big" house where another sister, Vera, who was married and lived in St Petersburg, often stayed.

After 1905 Mariamna and her husband Lev Alexeyevich lived for many years with their daughter Aliona in one of the smaller houses at Kamenka. Lev ran the estate and its sugar refinery, and gradually took over the whole enterprise. As early as 1906 Nicholas Vassilyevich made a will bequeathing the whole estate to him. In 1908 Lev bought another property, Dubrova, situated not far from Kamenka, and from that time on he, Mariamna and Aliona divided their time between Kamenka and Dubrova.

At the outbreak of war in 1914 Lev was mobilized, as were most of the men working on the various farms and estates of Kamenka. Mariamna and Aliona went to live in Kiev and when the bolsheviks overran the city they managed to reach Odessa. From there they went to Constantinople, then to Rome, and finally to Paris, where they lived until 1924 in very straitened circumstances. In 1924 they went to live in Concarneau, Brittany, where Mariamna's elder sister Juliet lived with her French husband and where both her parents were buried. In 1932 Mariamna returned to Paris and in 1949 she emigrated to the United States, where she died in 1961.

Since the original text of Mariamna's memoirs and all the watercolours had been destroyed in Russia before she left, she decided, while living in Concarneau, to reproduce them from memory for her granddaughter Irina, the daughter of Aliona. Her talent as a painter was such that she was able to capture in her watercolours the likeness of all the people she had known in Russia. She was intent on reproducing everything, down to the smallest details such as the design of the wallpaper, the fabric of the dresses or the material covering armchairs and sofas. She felt this was essential to convey what life had really been like in Russia before the Revolution among the families of well-to-do landowners and what the condition of the peasants and the servants had been. She left this wonderful heritage to her daughter, her granddaughter, and her great-grandchildren; and I am grateful to them for having agreed to let others share extracts from Mariamna's story through the publication of this book.

OLGA DAVYDOFF DAX

1 MATUSSOV

OUR HOUSE, a country estate called Matussov in the province of Kiev in southern Russia, was a splendid building, virtually a château and much too vast for our means. It required twelve servants to run it: six women and six men. The women slept in a large room next to my parents' bedroom and each had a small iron bed. The men slept downstairs as best they could, some behind a small curtain in the pantry and the younger ones on the floor.

During the day, the maintenance man, Zossim, often sat in a recess under the staircase (where he also slept), an enormous Book of Psalms open on his knees, reading and humming for hours; nobody ever interfered or reproached him for not working. Zossim was very pious.

My father's manservant, Matvei, was a small ageless man, always neatly turned out and ready to serve. He adored Papa and looked after him like a child, and when, after my father's death, my mother sold the estate and Matvei went back to his home in the village, he couldn't restrain himself from returning to the empty, abandoned château and cleaning father's room as he had always done, dusting and looking after the furniture as if my father were still alive.

In my childhood a chaplain officiated in the chapel that was part of the house, but as a result of the intrigues of a priest from another parish, the ecclesiastical authorities asked my parents to get rid of him. From then on very few services were celebrated in our chapel – only at Christmas, at Easter, and on the birthday of a member of the family.

In spite of this, Zossim would continue to put on the night-lights by the icons every Saturday evening, and when we walked by the chapel we would be frightened to see through the cloudy, wire-meshed windows those feeble lights that seemed to us like manifestations of the Great Beyond.

Zossim, our pious manservant, reading his Psalms in a niche under the
stairs and looking after the lamps

La chapelle du Château de Matoussof. Côté des maîtres.

Our private chapel at Matussov:

the family on one side, the servants on the other

As in every Russian country home, our bakery had a special importance. Baba Odarka, the bakerwoman, reigned supreme there. She baked fresh bread every day, but undertook a great many other tasks, particularly on holidays. She made delicate doughs that rose and fell at the slightest noise. The air was filled with the aromas of vanilla, cinnamon and lemon zest. A splendid plum cake stood next to brioches covered with sugar and almonds, and there were many other delicious things in preparation as Odarka kneaded a soft and pleasant swelling dough on the table.

The main courtyard of the house was followed by a succession of equally spacious courtyards, and off these were the outbuildings, the stables, the pigsty, the dairy, the store rooms, the cellars, etc. There were four separate wings, each consisting of six to eight rooms. The kitchen and the bakery were in one of these wings, in addition to a separate staff kitchen, and a sort of Turkish *hammam*. In my grandfather's day, the rooms in the other three wings were all for guests. He loved to entertain and would occasionally give sumptuous parties that lasted several days.

In my time, only one guest-room wing remained, and it was hardly ever used for that purpose because my parents almost never entertained. There was no superfluous luxury in our home, if one discounts the numerous domestics, the silverware on the immaculate tablecloth, and the four servants who waited at table. A strict etiquette prevailed: the children were not allowed to speak at table, and if one of us happened to bend forward Papa would strike the table with his hand, a reminder for us to keep our backs straight.

Other estates indulged in an overwhelming luxury; even in mid-winter, silver and vermeil vases were filled with lily-of-the-valley and roses. But Mama, who had always lived in the country, had her own ideas on these matters. Furthermore, she had been a young girl when the great reforms took place in Russia, and the emancipation of the serfs was proclaimed. Families like hers reduced their style of living; many even locked themselves in their houses and refused to entertain any more. Because of this, Mama grew up in straitened circumstances. When she married my father, Adrian Adrianovich Lopukhin, who was himself not well off, her dowry included a lovely estate near Matussov, where they settled down and lived as recluses.

When my mother's father died, his only son inherited the Matussov estate. He was a *bon vivant* who paid no attention to business and regarded his inheritance as nothing more than a means of acquiring ready money. The inevitable result was that he was forced to sell the property. My parents, who lived 15 km away, were the buyers.

Notre boulangère particulière.

Our bakery at Matussov, in the charge of Baba Odarka

La chambre des femmes de chambres

Our housemaids dealing with the linen on a wintry afternoon

ONE OF MAMA'S older sisters lived on an estate 50 km from Matussov, and this was one of the rare homes that we would visit. We used to be taken there, with the maids and governesses, once or twice a year in an omnibus that Papa had bought at Bellevolette's in Paris. Conrad, our confectioner, or Papa's valet Matvei sat next to the coachman. The trunks, and sometimes a young manservant or a chambermaid, sat on the upper deck. Mama, Papa, relatives or friends followed in victorias or coupés. The omnibus, drawn by six horses, advanced slowly because the tracks were often a sea of mud, and each time one of the travellers asked for something to eat or drink, or whatever, the whole caravan would come to a halt. At the halfway point there was a Jewish coaching inn where fresh horses, sent ahead the day before, were awaiting us. The servants brought out the hampers and then we would eat for two whole hours. One day we asked the innkeeper for borscht, the national soup of the Ukraine, and he brought us a chamberpot full of the delicious soup!

Our aunt's estate was like an oasis in the middle of the steppe. It was a lovely large house of red brick, surrounded by a huge park. In summer we would stop at the very end of the park and, while the coaches with the servants drove around it through the village, we would walk down the alley that led straight to the house.

The house had a huge lawn in front of it that sloped gently down to a pond, behind which the steppe extended into infinity. There were spacious rooms – a blue salon and a pink salon, a billiard room, an enormous dining room where, after each meal, a dwarf burnt perfume on a red-hot shovel. Aunt and Uncle had five daughters and one son who were our age, and there were masses of servants, maids and governesses, just as there were at Matussov.

Driving in the spring mud on a visit to our aunt's estate

Le Coiffeur en chef. – Avant Noël.

Conrad, our confectioner, performing one of his sweet miracles

A HUNDRED YEAR OLD mulberry tree with many trunks used to grow in front of the dining room windows. It was thick and stocky, with massive branches, one of which hung horizontally over the wide lane that bordered the house, and we loved to climb up it in summer.

Conrad, our confectioner, who had been a serf in his youth but was a white-haired old man by the time I knew him, would cook his jams most of the time under the mulberry tree.

Conrad was a real magician in his profession. He had been sent by my Orlov grandfather to train with the best confectioner in St. Petersburg. He came back a true expert in this art and his whole life long he stuffed my family with delicious pastries and sweets. In normal times he did the same chores as the other servants; only on great occasions, such as birthdays or holidays, would he disappear mysteriously into the kitchen to create his marvels. We would go secretly to watch him at work, licking our lips in anticipation at the

Conrad cooking jam under our old mulberry tree

The season called "gadanie",
when we picked branches from our cherry trees

sight of an almond-paste pyramid on the various levels of which appeared many diverse mushroom-shaped biscuits made of chocolate, sugared hazel nuts, caramelized nuts, *langues de chat*, patience dock leaves with aniseed . . . He also made all the jams, the crystallized fruit, and many other delicacies. He had a superb voice, a deep bass, and sang in the choir when there were services in the chapel.

O N 24 NOVEMBER, St. Catherine's day, we would rise before dawn, go out in the garden and pick branches of cherry trees, put them into a bottle filled with water, and make a wish, hoping that they would blossom before the 1st of January. If they did, the wish would be granted. . . . In fact, they blossomed only rarely; I have seen it happen only once or twice in my lifetime.

The days between 24 November and 6 January were known as "gadanie", which meant the time when one consulted the fates and drew lots by means of all sorts of witchcraft to guess the future and especially anything that had to do with love and marriage.

T HE MOST THRILLING PROCEDURE was the seance in the *hammam*. We never really had the courage to do it. One had to sit there with two lit candles between the two facing mirrors. They and the lights reflected from one to the other created a long corridor, at the end of which was supposed to appear the most significant event of the year. The apparition did not arrive right away. Often one had to wait for hours alone at night. Our chambermaids told us that some young girls had seen coffins and that they had died during the year; others had seen wedding processions and had married!

The *hammam* had been installed in time immemorial and though it was replaced by bathrooms it still had its advantages. On Saturdays the chambermaids came to fetch us and led us to the *hammam*. Outdoors was a wintry night. We crossed the courtyard, the snow crackling under our feet, the sky unfathomable and the stars shining and vibrating in the frozen air. When the door of the *hammam* was opened, clouds of steam poured out. One of the chambermaids sprayed the huge boiler with water, another prepared the basins for washing our hair, a third heated the towels.

The same winter picture awaited us on our way back to the main house: the hard menacing sky and the snow singing under our "valenkis" — felt-lined boots.

22

The hammam at Matussov

FOR AT LEAST the first ten years after Papa got into debt in order to buy Matussov, we suffered from a severe lack of money. This meant that we had nothing which had to be bought, such as new clothes or presents, and obviously no Christmas tree. There was a young mechanic working in our sugar factory, a Czech who, when he heard that we would have no Christmas tree, made one for us in the form of a pivoting tower that was rotated by the heat of the candles.

On Christmas Eve at about 5, the main salon was closed and we were forbidden to enter. It wasn't until much later, when we saw the rising of the first star in the icy cold sky, that we were invited to step into the salon. We stood on the threshold, filled with wonder and blinded by what was in the room. At first the candles on the mechanical tree prevented us from seeing anything but their flickering lights. Then, however, we began gradually to distinguish, on the platforms tapering upwards, animals, little men, birds, all in sugar or caramel. The mechanic who had created this looked at us with a gratified smile, pleased by the effect his work of art had had on us.

Un arbre de Noël mécanique et tournant.

The mechanical Christmas tree

AFTER THEIR MARRIAGE, neither of my parents ever really had fun out of life. As I and my sisters appeared, they became increasingly occupied with their large and time-consuming household. Nor did they ask anything more of life. Neither their isolated existence at Matussov nor the long winter months disturbed them. Mama could spend hours on end winding balls out of lamb's wool that had been spun by women in the village, and Papa would be downstairs in his study sculpting works of art in wood, making frames, boxes, etc. On the threshold of his study we would often see a Jew dressed in the traditional long frockcoat and with curls over his ears, negotiating for the wheat of the coming year, or testing the ground for the sale of old oxen or farm houses. "Well, Adrian Adrianovich," he would ask shyly, "how much wheat have you sown this year?"

Papa would blow away the shavings and sawdust from the wood, then mutter between two breaths, "Five hundred hectares." "Yes, I knew that already," said the Jew whose name was Yutka; "how much are you selling it for?" "Eighty kopecks," answered Papa. "I was told it was 79 kopecks," said Yutka, and Papa flew into a rage. But Yutka had already disappeared . . . which did not prevent him from returning the following day and many days after that, at the very same spot and asking exactly the same questions.

My parents had a number of pet occupations. Our courtyard was filled with carpenters, sculptors, blacksmiths who made all sorts of artistic objects under Papa's watchful eye – the "staircase of honour" with its carved banisters, wrought-iron lamp posts, and cupboards carved with designs taken from coloured albums Papa had brought back from Paris. Mama preferred living objects, animals of all sorts, and unfortunately she would get so absorbed by them that she tended to neglect me and my sisters in both our emotional and our psychological development.

We were very pious and as long as our priest, Father Nicholas, who was paid by us, conducted his services in our chapel we attended regularly. Mama, who loved music and had a good voice, had organized a choir, in which the principal singers were Conrad (bass), Zossim (an insignificant tenor), and another servant, Effim (a superb tenor). Mama was the soprano and a number of local boys completed the choir. The rehearsals took place in the large circular salon and were a real treat for us. We listened as in a trance but were not allowed to take part.

Le studio de mon père Adrien Lopoukhine.

Papa in his study

THE CHURCH of the Ascension was 3 km from Matussov. Its priest, Father Agathon, was said to be the offspring of one of grandfather Orlov's escapades with a gypsy woman. Whether this was true or not, we loved him very much.

It was not often that we were taken to church, especially in winter when it was feared that we might catch cold. But since it was compulsory at the great holy days, we stood in church on the clear and cold morning of December 25th. There was a lot of snow that winter and the church windows were all frosty and blue. We sat in our usual pews on the left and looked at the other people, the young peasant girls with their heads covered in flowers and ribbons, the police representative straight and solemn in his ceremonial suit, and some unknown people in the choir on the right. They looked like strangers, for their clothes were different from those we were used to seeing. After a moment's thought we came to the conclusion that they must be Father Agathon's children.

The service comes to an end. People start leaving and Mama wishes to speak to Father Agathon. She moves close to the altar and we wait there among freezing gusts for him to appear. Ah! Here he is at last, with a smile on his lips. Mama asks him to come the following evening to say vespers at our home at 6 and mass the day after that in our chapel. Out of the corner of our eyes we see the strangers stepping down from the choir. "Here are my children," stutters Father Agathon, "step forward, step forward . . . th . . . th . . . they have come for the feast fr . . . fr . . . from Kiev. Sasha, Yulya . . . There you are!"

We and the children gawk at each other. Mama says, "So that's decided for tomorrow evening!"

We leave the church and climb into our sleighs. We are all wrapped up in furs. It is a glorious day, sparkling with frost, about 10 degrees below zero.

Tired of waiting, the horses gallop off on the snowpath. We look back to see "the children" again, walking in Indian file behind their father along the wooden palisade that borders the presbytery garden.

Father Agathon conducting Christmas mass in the Church of the Ascension

THE NEXT EVENING Father Agathon duly arrives at our chapel in a horse-drawn sleigh. The small bell starts ringing under the watchful hand of Zossim to announce the start of the service.

Our seats are on the left, facing the altar. On the right are the choirboys who have been joined by Conrad, Effim, Zossim and Mama. They bend over a yellow-leaved book and by the light of a wax candle decipher Slavonic letters as they sing psalms.

When the service comes to an end the good Father goes up to Mama, and she asks him to bring some of his children to mass tomorrow. And so the next morning we gather again for mass. Father Agathon appears through the central door, holding a gold cup in his hands. This is the moment for communion. "This is the flesh and the blood of Our Lord Jesus Christ," he proclaims.

After mass, the priests and the choirboys hasten to the out-buildings where a meal awaits them. The deacon is taken by Conrad and Zossim to the pantry where he is offered coffee. Father Agathon and his sons are invited to the house where coffee is served, with biscuits and cakes on a beautiful silver tray.

The young men say Thank you and we take them to another room to get better acquainted. They are so nice in their navy blue uniforms with silver buttons. Palya especially is a very handsome boy; he must be about 14. They are thoughtful and sociable; they talk, tell stories, and even sing "Drink some Tokay wine and your heart will be merry." They are the first young men we have ever met, and we are all aflutter at the sight of Palya's sky-blue eyes. He tells us that they are five girls and five boys.

In the main salon Father Agathon is preparing to leave and calls his sons. "So it's agreed," he says to Mama. "At the New Year m..m..my children will be expecting . . ."

They have hardly left when we pounce on Mama. "What is happening for the New Year? Are you taking us to church? What will the children be expecting? Please tell us, Mama!" And she finally says that we are invited to spend the afternoon at the presbytery. We go mad with joy at this news, we shout and dance. At last we are going to meet them all!

It was bitterly cold at the New Year. The whole of nature seemed petrified by frost. The smoke rose from the cottages straight and blue, as if motionless in the light grey velvety and opaque sky, as in a Japanese drawing. Covered in bear and wolf furs we drove in a sleigh to Father Agathon's presbytery.

It resembled a cottage but was much larger. As we approached it seemed to be sunk in the snow, its windows only 75 cm above the ground. Generally speaking, the priests in the Ukraine were very well off because the peasants in their parishes were prosperous. Thus

Father Agathon having coffee in our house

Christmas carols outside Father Agathon's snow-covered presbytery

Father Agathon owned cows, pigs, good horses, coaches, servants, and even a 500-hectare estate, 20 km from Matussov, with a nice house and outbuildings.

We were not the only guests that New Year's Day. There were other priests, some with their families, others with only their wives, who sat in a row under the icons, drinking one glass of tea after another. We young ones were piled up in the girls' room where narrow iron beds were lined up against the walls. Father Agathon's children were entertaining us: Palya sang, Petya played the fool, pretty Sasha with the curly golden hair laughed with my sister Juliet while I philosophized with Yulya. "Everyone in the dance room," rang out a voice in the doorway and Masha appeared striking her hands. "We are going to dance," she said laughingly and pushed us out of the overheated room one after another. She was a student at the Moscow Conservatory and already played the piano beautifully. Masha played a furious waltz while couples took to the floor that had been waxed to make it more slippery. Every minute servants passed around trays of candies, chocolates, caramels, nuts, figs, dates, pistachios, hazel nuts, gingerbread, crystallized fruits . . . We had never been to such a party!

Mama visiting in Father Agathon's house

Bal chez le prêtre le père Agathon.

Marie Nikolaievna

A dance at Father Agathon's

WE HAD NICKNAMED HIM Chikotini, an italianized name for a consumptive. He was a schoolteacher and also head of the choir in Father Agathon's church. He was a very good musician, and naturally I became his sentimental victim. My love lasted several years; the charm of Panthelemon (his real name) was that he corresponded exactly to the type of sweetheart I dreamed of. He was young, tall, thin and fair (at least that was how I saw him), and above all he was consumptive! He was nervous and jumpy, and each time he started coughing he raised his hands to his head or his chest, which always caused me great emotion. I was filled with joy when, after giving the pitch, he extended his hands and gave the choir the signal to begin a psalm or a prayer, his foot beating time.

This crush of mine was touching and at the same time comical. It was closely linked to our visits to church and to Father Agathon's family. When we went horseback riding we would always try to pass next to the presbytery and would cast tender looks at the cottage next door, which was the school where Chikotini lived. When services took place in our chapel, Chikotini would come over the day before with his choirboys to rehearse with Mama. We listen enthralled to the religious songs led by *his* expert hands. I only had eyes for *him* in his rather overlong frockcoat, totally immersed in his art.

We never spoke to each other, not ever, but what did that matter?

Répétition avec la maîtrise. Tchikotini.

My first crush, the schoolteacher Chikotini, with the choirboys

Natoulia.

In our childhood, governesses came and went with noticeable speed. Entire months would elapse without Mama being able to find one willing to come and work in our "hole". Up to the end of our schooling we had twenty-five of them in all.

One was named Natulia Bernadsky. She was a splendid girl of 16 whose father, a doctor, had begged Mama to take her, "to hide her", he said, because she was so beautiful. She was supposed to give us lessons but at 9 we would still be waiting for her; she liked to stay in bed until 10.

In the autumn, Mama's brother, Uncle David Orlov, arrived for the hunting season. He was a jolly little man with fiery eyes in a handsome face, a spendthrift and a philanderer. He was an officer of His Majesty the Emperor's Cossacks, and he was struck by Natulia's beauty. One morning when the men prepared to leave for the hunt, they were just settling into the coaches in front of the porch and the servants were bringing the hampers, when Natulia rushed out on the balcony overlooking the porch and poured a jar of water onto Uncle David's head. In a rage he rushed up the stairs, seized Natulia in his arms and boorishly kissed her a dozen times, then ran back down as fast as he could, leaving the young girl entirely confused, scarlet and upset to the verge of tears. In spite of this, she continued to tease him. One day he put a cigarette out in her ear. Shortly afterwards Mama asked her father to take her back.

Ida was small and round with an alarming face. As soon as our homework and lessons were over, she would be off to the village and stay there for hours. She was silent and mysterious, but Mama learnt that during her daily absences she would visit peasants and preach Marxism, which we called nihilism, to them. She did not last long after that.

Lady Charlotte was disfigured, a hunchback as the result of a case of tuberculosis (or perhaps scarlet fever) when she was 7. When still an adolescent, she left her large family in England and travelled in many countries, ending up in Russia with the idea of teaching English to children. She worked first for my mother's sister, Princess Sophia Kudachev, and then came to us. She taught us French and English, and was gentle, gay and subtle, unlike Mama or the other governesses who lost patience and punished us. She always wore black satin dresses with a long train, a bonnet made of black lace that fell down over her poor hump, and a chinpiece.

Lady Charlotte distribue des récompences pour des réponses bien faites aux leçons.

Three of our many governesses: Natulia, Ida and Lady Charlotte

Ida la gouvernante nihiliste.

AT EPIPHANY, on January 6th, we were invited to the presbytery for an afternoon and evening dance. After mass everyone, the priest and the choir in the lead, banners in front, went to the pond to bless the water. The priest said prayers at the foot of a big cross hewn out of the ice, then plunged a silver cross into the pond and gave the blessing.

Since our first meeting with Father Agathon's children we had become better acquainted and we felt totally at ease with them. I never stopped dancing with his son Petya, who claimed to be in love with me.

We stayed for dinner, which was served on long narrow tables. The meal was varied and copious, and lots of vodka was drunk. The borscht was fatty and rich. The priests, bent very low over the table, lapped it up with relish. It ran down their beards and their moustaches dipped into it. After the zakusky and the borscht we were served with many sorts of fish with salted cucumbers, marinated fruits and apple preserved in a special brine: then came the turn of the roast, chicken, turkey, goose with apples, followed by a dessert and oranges, tea with cakes and pastries. Two full hours were spent at the table, and the ball lasted until midnight.

IT IS THE BEGINNING of Lent. The snow is grey and so are the days. We wander in the park, caught up in a wave of poetic melancholy, searching with our feet for last year's blackened leaves.

The seven weeks of Lent always marked our lives. The first week everyone fasted. We were allowed no meat, no eggs, no butter and for some people even no sugar. For us Lent symbolized the awakening of nature, the tender spring that followed the long cold months of bad weather and a closed-in existence in overheated and unventilated rooms.

During Holy Week we would perform our Easter duties at Father Agathon's, and we waited impatiently for that moment to come. In the meantime we roamed dreamily in the park looking for the first violet. At 4, the bells started ringing in all the churches, calling the faithful to Confession. There they were, trudging along in the mud, lifting their booted feet with difficulty out of the sticky compost.

Holy Thursday was the opening day of the series of great religious services that marked Passion Week. We spent the whole day waiting for the evening service when Father Agathon, in a solemn atmosphere, would read twelve passages from the Gospels on the Passion of Jesus Christ.

We gulped our food down as soon as we heard the sound of the coach outside. Then we piled into the "lineika", a wide carriage with several seats. The horses advanced at a walking pace, slipping as they sank into the black mud.

The church was packed. It was the custom to burn candles during the reading of the Gospels; each person had his own and they lit up the whole church. Here was Father Agathon coming from the altar to read and the divine words vibrated in the overheated atmosphere, blurred in the clouds of incense and faded away in the thick shadows of the high cupola.

Nous allons aux douzes Evangils le Jeudi Saint.

Going to the Church in the evening on Holy Thursday

BETWEEN MIDNIGHT MASS on Easter eve and the early morning service, the faithful went home to fetch their Easter fare – the dyed eggs, the roasted suckling pig, the sausages, the cream cheese, the cakes, etc. – which they placed around the church so that the priest could bless it all after the service. This was the age-old custom.

We remained waiting in the church because the priest was coming to our home to bless the already laden table. We waited about one and a half hours, chatting softly in the church that had become dark and silent.

At last the service began again. We were tired. The big windows became bluish and the service ended. We went out, banners leading the way. "Christ is risen! Christ is risen!" burst out everywhere. The peasants appeared in a violet pink glow around the church and were immediately blessed by Father Agathon. He was dressed in silver and gold lamé, and enveloped in the blue smoke from his censer.

We returned home in the cold morning air to find a fragrant coffee awaiting us in the dining room. We ate cakes as daylight gazed at us through the windows on this glorious day of Resurrection. Then we went to bed and slept until one.

Easter Sunday was beautiful, mild and sunny. We spent it loafing around the park or around the Easter table. Finally Nicholas Nicholaevich, the son of our current governess, suggested he read us a short tale he had written. He took us out into the park, and sat Juliet and me on a bench while he sat on the ground amid the flowers and read to us. He put so much feeling into his reading that we were filled with enthusiasm. I was even more moved than Juliet because from the start of his Easter visit Nicholas had singled me out from the rest of my sisters. His little black eyes were always searching for me, observing me. I couldn't guess the meaning of all this, but his continual little game was far from displeasing me, since I did not dislike him at all.

On the day when Nicholas was leaving he came up to me, took me by the arm, and said, "Come with me." I felt my arm gripped tightly, and all of a sudden he bent down and pressed his lips passionately on my hand!

I thought for weeks afterwards that I was in love with him. But since I knew it could never lead to a "proper" marriage, I gradually drove him out of my mind and developed other crushes.

La bénédiction du pain pascal à la fin de la messe de Minuit de Pâques.

The outdoor blessing service after midnight mass

THE WINTER OF 189- ended with a great sadness. In early January, my sister Varinka fell ill. It was diagnosed as typhoid, and in March she died. This calamity had a disastrous effect on Mama. Throughout the year, Mama's grief seemed to get worse daily. She gave up all her occupations and lay in bed for hours suffering from severe migraine, or else she remained distant and indifferent to everything. We had to convince Papa that she urgently needed to be amused, to divert her mind from her grief and to let her develop new ideas. Towards the autumn our plans ripened and we finally decided to spend the winter in no less a place than Paris.

Slowly Mama began to wake up out of her lethargy and to come back to life. That was in November. We needed clothes for the journey, so Mama left one evening for Kiev. On the day of her return, announced as usual by a telegram, we were all agog even at 8 in the morning though we knew perfectly well that she could not possibly arrive until 11. We rushed upstairs with a telescope to scan the road. At last the coach appeared, all muddy with steaming horses!

What wonderful things Mama had bought! Unfortunately everything was either black or dark grey, but it didn't matter, it was for Paris! In no time at all the materials she had chosen were transformed into dresses, blouses, coats, by a Jewish tailor from a nearby village.

The journey was quite comical. Mama, who had not left the country for thirty years except for short visits to Kiev, remembered foreign trains as being unheated, so she dressed us up as if we were going to the North Pole with red flannel pants, gaiters, fur-lined galoshes and warm petticoats. Once on the overheated train, we started peeling off the various layers one by one.

Mama had also said that the trains travelled so fast that there was no time to buy anything in the stations so she brought along a large hamper filled with food. To our surprise, we discovered that, as we were in first class international trains, we had access to a magnificent dining car that followed us all the way to Paris. But we had to eat our own food from the hamper!

Nous partons pour Paris!!!

Our departure for Paris

FOR OUR THIRD WINTER in Kiev, Mama rented a superb apartment, with a large dancing room and dining room. We gave several parties there, but we were short of young men, so a friend suggested that we invite Lev Davydoff, a young cavalry officer who was on leave following an accident in which he had almost been killed. Tall, handsome, fair-haired and a very good dancer, he came to our parties, but we snubbed him a little because we felt sorry for our own young men who looked so insignificant compared to him.

When we returned to the country we got to know Lev's sister, Tassya, who was a charming young girl, the opposite of her brother, with very dark hair and a dark complexion, shrewd but always ready to laugh, and kind. Naturally Lev was also there and he used to come and see us often.

IN THE SPRING and summer of 1899, Lev Davydoff and I saw each other again. He and his sister were constantly organizing picnics, either in Trostianka, a small wood near Kamenka, or in the Big Wood.

One day we went to have tea at Trostianka, and Lev, lying flat on his stomach at my feet, told me so many stupid things that I disliked him intensely. When he suggested that he come with me in my carriage I refused. Tassya laughed at this and I became annoyed, but in spite of the fact that Lev had a confused and disappointed mien I refused to go with him.

As the days passed, however, I thought more and more of him, and missed his company when he was absent.

In September the hunting season began. I went to one of these hunts on a beautiful, calm and golden day. The fallen leaves that formed a Persian carpet under one's feet smelt of musk.

At lunch I sat next to my cousin Marguerite, who must have noticed that I was sad because Lev was not there. She said to me, "Why don't you marry your Levuchka, he is so sweet!" I jumped and mumbled rather bitterly, "But does he like me?" "I think so," she answered.

Two days later I went to see Tassya in the big house. We were sitting together in one of the small rooms when the door suddenly burst open and Lev appeared in full uniform, looking very thin and handsome. I asked why he had lost so much weight and he answered, "Because I have been thinking of you!" Tassya wanted to leave, but he held her back.

The day passed without my realizing it. In the early evening, after a walk and dinner, I went out of doors and sat on a bench. Lev followed and sat next to me. Taking my hand, he

The winter season is here

The modest home of Lev's mother in Kiev

said in a voice choked with emotion, "I must say something to you." "Say what?" I asked him teasingly. "No, not here," he said, looking towards the house. "Let's go for a walk."

We rose and walked in silence through the courtyard and down a staircase hung over with motionless, yellowing leaves mixed with bright red Virginia creeper. The leaves smelled of amber, that special aroma of a damp September night.

At the crossing of the first alley, Lev took my hand. "This is what I wanted to say to you. I love you and if you agree we will never leave each other . . ."

We stopped in the small narrow lane. My heart was beating in my throat and I whispered, "I agree, but we must speak about it to Mama."

He embraced me. I turned my head and he kissed my forehead. We went quickly back to the house where all the windows and doors on the garden side were open.

A picnic in the woods; Lev lies at my feet

THE WEDDING was fixed for the 12th of November. Mama and I went to Kiev to order my trousseau, which was very modest because we had little money. Two dozen slips, two nightdresses, two dozen underdrawers, two dozen black silk stockings, two dozen lisle ones, three or four dresses, one pelisse, one otterskin *chapka* with a blue ribbon, two dozen sheets and six pillowcases, table cloths, flower baskets and many sprays of lilac. We called on Lev's mother, Maria Nikolaevna, and left the trousseau there, because Lev and I would have to go through Kiev on our way to Petersburg after the wedding.

Invitations were sent out, and we spent the remaining weeks working out all the details. Two or three days before the wedding, we started to prepare the food, to carve the veal and the lamb. Conrad was busy making various sorts of biscuits, tarts and elaborate sweets.

On the evening of November 11th, Father Agathon said vespers in our church while Lev and I and a friend sat in the big hall and played Makao. It was only at the end of the service that we abandoned our card game and went to church to see what was going on, because after all the service was for us! The servants and villagers lined the walls, and at the far end the iconostasis shone by the light of the candles and the red lanterns. Our old retainer Zossim read in a thin voice the first verse of a hymn.

November 12th is a grey day, gloomy and rainy. The house is packed with people. I come downstairs for lunch but don't feel like talking to anyone. The sooner the ceremony is over, the sooner Lev and I will be alone. My friends dress me to be ready at 3 o'clock. One of them sets the veil and the flowers. I have a wonderful damask printed dress with a long train.

I walk down the big staircase to the hall where all my friends are waiting. I enter the church on Papa's arm. Lev in his white cavalry jacket is waiting, anxious and handsome. The church is full. I am the first to set foot on the satin of the lectern. Everything goes well after all – that is to say, the way things should go for a wedding!

After dinner, at 9, we go to the Tsvetkov station, 8 versts away. Finally we are alone in our own railway coach. Only the conductor comes to ask us if we need anything. I put on my lovely new blue dressing gown and undo my hair. At last alone.

The day of my wedding

38   1899   Mam Leslie   Kasotchka

1899

Our first apartment: Tsarskoye Selo

LEV AND I TRAVELLED from Kiev to Petersburg, where we had to wait half an hour for the train to Tsarskoye Selo, where we would be living. We had taken a maid, Masha, with us, a spinster who cried all day long. Lev's coachman was waiting for us at the station and took care of the luggage while we climbed onto a one-horse sleigh and started off for home. It was snowing hard and the "sleigh lane" was already open.

Our apartment looked delightful. A table covered in cream cretonne with large artificial carnations stood in the middle of the drawing room on a red woollen carpet. On the lovely desk near the table was a small vase of scented artificial flowers. One of the doors of the drawing room gave on to Lev's office, the other on to a cloakroom that led to the dining room.

The feeling of being my own mistress was quite new to me, and I never forgot it for the rest of my life. The smooth sheets, the down pillows covered in yellow atlas piqué pillowcases with flounces, the blankets . . . oh, how wonderful it all was! And a husband! This was for me a brand new country, so different from our own Little Russia – other people, Lev's regiment, his interests, his life . . . It was so great a change for me that it made my head spin. I felt drunk and my life seemed to be a fairy tale.

OFTEN TWO of Lev's friends, Gor and Chal, would arrive in town. I believe they worked in some ministry or other. We liked them both very much, and I particularly liked Gor, who was very handsome and elegant. He tried to court me, but I was not ready for that!

After lunch Lev ordered that his horse Vikhr be harnessed in such a way that Gor could slip the reins around his waist, install himself on skis, and ride in this fashion around the parks of Pavlovsk and Tsarskoye Selo.

WHEN WE RETURNED from Matussov we brought back an adorable foal which we named Julik – meaning "rogue" – and we bought from Mitya two very young mares – Veda and Vakhanka – so that when we arrived in Tsarskoye Selo we owned a team of three horses. Lev then bought a large sleigh with bells. How wonderful this all was! Though they were not big, the horses were as fast as arrows. It was very difficult to stop them when they raced down avenues and lanes, and we had to keep our eyes open. One even had great difficulty in simply directing them. They never slowed down in curves and Lev would

Gor riding around the park, harnessed to our horse Vikhr

almost fall out of the sleigh as he endeavoured to counterbalance its weight to prevent it from overturning. Calm and phlegmatic, Miron simply held the reins!

We had a lot of incidents with these horses. One day Miron was hitching them up and let go of them for barely a second to take his gloves. They promptly sprang away in the courtyard and galloped out into the street where they raced along between the lamp-posts. They finally struck one of the lamp-posts, which broke Julik's harness, and she rolled like a ball on the sidewalk. The two other horses were unable to negotiate the next curve and came to a halt in front of the house that stood on the corner where Lev, Miron and I, who had run after them, found them and brought them home with no further trouble – but with a broken bridle and a torn harness.

2 Kamenka

Our troika at Tsarskoye Selo

IN 1902 ALIONA WAS BORN, and two days later Lev was given command of the Fourth Squadron, the very one he had served in. He had to learn his new job and deal with the officers on a different footing. During that winter we had been told that Papa's business affairs were going badly but he never spoke of it when he came to visit. Finally Mama informed us that she could no longer send us any money, things were so bad.

I had already been hinting, and indeed saying aloud, that Lev should leave his regiment and devote his strength and energy to better things. He would always reply that one had to have something else in view before taking such a decision. So I wrote to the vice-governor of Warsaw, Krevsky, who was married to the sister of a good friend of ours. He promised to give Lev a post as regional director. From that moment I decided to leave Tsarskoye Selo for ever and went to Kamenka with Aliona. In August 1903 we received a letter from Krevsky informing us that Lev had been named regional director for the Polish town of Wloclawek, in the province of Warsaw, one hour by road from the German border of Alexandrov/Thorn. Lev returned to Tsarskoye Selo in the autumn to relinquish his command and to pack our belongings.

Russian social life in a garrison town like Wloclawek was entirely new to me. All its principles, its views, its customs were the direct opposite of all I had seen until then. Most of the people were of very modest status, never left Wloclawek and mixed only with one another. Flirtations were common and went very far without causing either embarrassment or shame. Neither husbands nor wives paid any attention and their habits were extremely dissolute.

JULY 1905! Russia is drifting! Something is going wrong with the Russo-Japanese war. *Liberation* publishes articles that are increasingly fiery. Lev says that even in Wloclawek there are revolutionaries who are going around disseminating proclamations and calling for strikes.

One day the local factories went on strike and a crowd of workers marched on the town hall. Lev rode on his horse Vikhr into the crowd and tried to convince them to disperse, but nobody listened to him and the crowd grew larger. A detachment of soldiers, led by a young officer, appeared through the crowded streets.

The workmen, 5,000 of them, blocked the street for three whole days, during which the local citizens trembled for fear of brigandry. They finally came to an agreement with the factory managers, a resolution was passed that seemed to satisfy everyone, and the strike

The aunts' house at Kamenka

ended. A few days later Lev received a letter from the governor, congratulating him for having controlled the strike in such a diplomatic manner. This was most agreeable, and we decided there and then to go to Kamenka.

UNCLE NICHOLAS Vassilyevich lived in a house called the Green House, which stood in the middle of a small garden, and his two sisters, "the aunts", lived in another house where we were put up when we arrived from Wloclawek. Our description of the strike made a great impression on everyone. The aunts uttered ohs! and ahs!, and Uncle Nicholas repeatedly said, "Bravo! Bravo! So you were not scared! I am very pleased!"

However, the railroad strike that followed shook us. As our leave ended in October, we still hoped to return to Wloclawek by the last train before the strike. We were driven to the station in a carriage drawn by four white horses while Vassya, one of Lev's cousins, who was almost always drunk, galloped around the coach firing a revolver in the air. We were still some distance from the station when we saw the train was ready to leave. Vassya galloped off to make it wait for us; but fate willed otherwise. The train left without us and we had to return to Kamenka. (We learned a short time later that it had only been able to go as far as Brest, where it was forced to stop because the railway strike had begun!)

What luck that we had missed it! Furthermore, the next day Alionushka fell seriously ill. We were very worried about Lev's leave and feared it would not be extended. In the evenings we remained in the dining room watching Varya tie jampots while Tassya sewed a blouse, the sleeve of which she had accidentally cut off because she was so troubled by a telegram she received from her suitor Petya Ryjov.

During the three weeks we were forced to stay in Kamenka we received no letters or newspapers, and during those weeks our future was decided. Uncle Nicholas lost his two most faithful servants: the manager Gubert, who took another job, and the accountant Plessky, who, after working for Uncle Nicholas for over fifty years, was virtually abducted by the Davydoffs of Yurchikha. Thus Uncle Nicholas found himself alone. Lev suggested that he stay on to help him, to which the old man answered, "Thank you, Lev. Please do and get down to work right away!"

Ж.Д забастовка в Октябрь 1905 года в Каменкъ.

Время препровожденіе во время забастовки

Sitting together in the kitchen at Kamenka waiting for news of the railway strike.
Tassya is sewing a blouse, Varvara is tying jam pots

THE EXQUISITE LIFE that Kamenka had known when it was filled with people was a thing of the distant past. Its guiding spirit now was Uncle Nicholas. At 18 he had joined the Preobrazhensky Regiment and one day, during an important parade, the Emperor had noticed him as a new man and asked who he was. When told that it was Davydoff, son of the Decembrist exile, the Emperor said, "So that is why he stares at me like a wolf!" This remark so offended Uncle Nicholas, whose eyes were indeed serious and unsmiling, but who felt nothing but loyalty to the Tsar, that he resigned and retired to the country for good, in order to straighten out the estate that had been woefully neglected by his tutors during his minority. He finally made enough money to give each of his sisters and brothers (there were ten of them) a sum on which they could live. Most of them would come and stay in Kamenka as long as they wished, the married ones with their families.

Lev's father, Alexis Vassilyevich, who enjoyed the good life, had quickly spent his capital, so that his children had to be brought up mainly in Kamenka.

The Decembrist's family returning from their Siberian exile in a "tarantass", a huge carriage which had difficulty climbing the steep hills

THE AUNTS' HOUSE was a low, but quite large one-storey building with a green roof. The rooms were medium-sized but numerous and divided into two lots by a long corridor where later, during the long winter evenings, Lev and I liked to stroll while discussing the day's events.

At this time we occupied two tiny rooms in the left wing, where we worried about extended leave and dreamt of staying in Kamenka forever. Shivering in our cold beds, we asked ourselves what would happen if Lev stayed to run the estate and what Uncle Nicholas would do about his will.

When I became a part of Kamenka, Uncle Nicholas, Aunt Sasha, Aunt Lisa and Aunt Vera were living there. The aunts were educated ladies, quiet, kind and well brought up, who were always together, either sitting and reading or looking after sick peasants. Aunt Lisa, who was forceful and quick-tempered, would occasionally show her displeasure, but she was always fair and thoughtful. She loved her little dog, which she always held on her lap.

Aunt Sasha, the youngest of the three, remembered Siberia where she was born, and her father during his exile, whereas Aunt Lisa, who was born before her father was deported, had stayed in Russia. That is probably why Aunt Sasha had a somewhat sad look about her.

During the last years of his exile, her father Vassily Lvovich fell ill and became progressively weaker. Aunt Sasha would read to him. He was a very serious and intelligent man and he owned a large number of books that had been sent to him from Paris by his relatives the de Gramonts.

Aunt Sasha was very close to her parents. She was approximately 20 when her mother returned from Siberia with the children. Alexander II had amnestied the Decembrists when he became Tsar, but Vassily Lvovich died before this great day and the family left Krasnoyarsk without being aware of the amnesty. They only learned about it when, in one of the railway stations of Siberia, they ran into Prince Volkonsky, who was bringing the Tsar's manifesto, and this meeting was a very sad and touching one.

NICHOLAS VASSILYEVICH never married and never left Kamenka. He was a very robust man until he was 75. Short but thickset, he had severe eyes which frightened most people a little; but he spoke slowly and precisely in a pleasant and friendly tone of voice.

Though he never married he was not averse to mistresses; I was told that Ivan the gardener would act as his intermediary and bring home young girls. It was said that he had

Uncle Nicholas with Aunt Sasha and Aunt Lisa; Lev and I are strolling in the corridor

many children in the village, but he was always very generous with his mistresses when he left them and saw to it that they married well. In the last half of his life he lived with one of his laundresses, a beautiful Polish girl by whom he had a daughter, Varvara Nikolaevna, who went to live with her mother when she married. Later he had an affair with a girl who worked in the garden; she gave birth to a boy who died in infancy, and two girls, Nina Nikolaevna and Manya Nikolaevna.

At about this time one of Uncle Nicholas's brothers, Lev Vassilyevich, who had married Tchaikovsky's sister, Alexandra Ilyinishna, arrived in Kamenka and Uncle Nicholas took him on as manager of the estate. Alexandra Ilyinishna, a charming and endearing woman, had a great influence on her brother-in-law. Around 1873 her kindness and sympathy for him led her to try and build a family around him for his old age, and indeed she convinced him to adopt his eldest daughter Varvara Nikolaevna, and to install his last mistress and her daughters in more comfortable surroundings. This all happened, and of course it could not fail to scandalize certain members of the family, in particular Aunt Sasha. It was said that she never altogether forgave him. As long as Uncle Nicholas's affairs remained secret everyone was content, but when he installed his mistress openly for all to see, and went regularly to her home for tea at 5, it was not to be unexpected that everyone should feel outraged.

What pleasure it was for him to take tea in summer in the small wing of his mistress's house! Simple plates and a boiling samovar were set on the table. Standing in front of her master, the sweet and tender woman, with submissive blue eyes, would pour his tea. I can describe her because I was told that Nina looked like her.

When she was later married off, for reasons that I don't know, the two small girls moved into the big house to live with the aunts. Aunt Lisa took sides with Nicholas Vassilyevich and launched into the education of his daughters. A short while later they also took in Varvara Nikolaevna. The small house in the big garden was cleaned up, the office was moved there, and the children, who had forgotten their earlier life, became an integral part of Kamenka.

By 1899, when I arrived in Kamenka, Varvara and Nina had already married. Only Manya, frail and always ill, sad and discontented, never married, so she grew up without a name and no assurance of her future. It was only during our time there that Uncle Nicholas adopted her legally and gave her the name of Davydoff.

Uncle Nicholas (with Lev at his side) and his three illegitimate daughters: Varvara, Manya and Nina

THE PLESSKY AFFAIR concerns the Davydoff family who lived at Yurchikha, 3 versts from Kamenka. Uncle Nicholas's brother, Pyotr Vassilyevich, had had one son, Vassily Petrovich, who married Princess Olga Alexandrovna Lieven and lived in Yurchikha. They had three sons before Vassily died insane. His widow, an embittered woman, enormously fat, dark-skinned, mannish and rough, was devoted only to her sons Vassya, Petya and Sasha, and intended for one of them to inherit the whole Kamenka estate when Uncle Nicholas died. Aware of Plessky's influence on Uncle Nicholas, she built all her hopes on him to achieve her object, and she began to visit his office with noticeable frequency.

One day, when Lev was absent, she came to the office and a serious talk took place between her and Plessky. The latter got very excited, and when Lev arrived as the end of their conversation he was surprised to see Plessky twirling his cane in front of Olga Alexandrovna's nose and shouting, "I have a cane with two ends!" Olga Alexandrovna got up immediately with an outraged look and left the house. Lev had no idea what they had been arguing about, but did his best to calm Plessky down. Two or three hours later, however, two red-faced and grim-looking horsemen with whips in their hands appeared in Kamenka. They were Olga's sons Vassya and Petya. They went first to the office, but were told that Plessky was with Uncle Nicholas. They hurried over to the house and stood waiting in the courtyard. When Plessky eventually emerged from the house, they went up to him, one on each side, their whips twirling and whistling in the air. They told him in a nasty and menacing manner: "You are going to come with us right now and apologize to our mother for the horrid things you said to her this morning!"

The old man started to tremble at the thought of going into the den of these ruffians. His small grey beard shook and his face lost all its dignity and stoicism. He refused point blank to go with them, saying he had no reason to apologize, and walked off as fast as he could. He fled to the nearby aunts' house, but not before Petya's whip, whistling around his head, struck him painfully on the back. In a second he had disappeared inside the house and hid behind a screen near a wash-basin; sitting on the bidet, he never stopped howling.

The brothers dashed off furiously to the village where they managed to get roaring drunk. From time to time they returned to the house and bellowed for Plessky. It was not till 1 a.m. that Plessky decided to rise from the bidet, ordered us to take some pikes which the guards used and accompany him to the room by the kitchen. The next morning when Lev went to see how he had spent the night, he was nowhere to be found. At 4 in the morning he had ordered the four-horse coach to be got ready, and had been driven to the station, not at Kamenka but at Raygorod. There he disappeared completely and for ever!

Poor terrified Plessky, barely able to walk, as we prop him up and carry protective pikes in our hands

WHEN LEV TOOK OVER management of the estate, it was divided into three farming enterprises: the Nikolaevsky, the Pliakovsky and the Podlesnoe, which included the Lesnichestva and comprised some 2,000 *dessiatines*. Everything was in perfect condition but run in a rather old-fashioned way. Lev started making his way modestly. He had a great deal of patience and intuition. In the office he listened to the old servants, learning and informing himself from them.

At the end of October the railway strike came to an end and we left by the first available train for Wloclawek, Lev to settle his affairs and Tassya and I to gather our effects and furniture and send them to Kamenka.

On the long journey we arrived one day at noon at a village where we were supposed to have lunch and feed the horses. We walked into an inn, all dark and warm inside. We ordered a samovar, which in no time at all was steaming and singing on our table. The door opened softly and the yellowish and taciturn face of the innkeeper appeared. He asked us if we wished to hear a harpist who sang traditional Polish songs. The musician was a little old man with thick hair as light and soft as a swan's feathers, clean-shaven except for a moustache. We ate and drank while he played and sang for us. I don't remember ever having heard anything more poetic and original. His old fingers were still able to pluck the strings with agility and his cracked, frail voice expressed a whole range of emotions.

When it was time to move on, the harpist followed us out of the inn, raising his hat every minute and thanking us with a winning smile for the generosity of our tip.

During our brief stay in Wloclawek, which was virtually in a state of war, Lev was able to resign his post, and Tassya and I packed all our belongings. Finally, on 30 November 1905, we were back in peaceful, beloved Kamenka, our new home.

UPON OUR RETURN from Wloclawek, we had to borrow money immediately. The house that had been allotted to us was called the "doctorate" and stood right by the wall of the big courtyard on the other side of the road – in truth, in the village itself. We moved in just before Christmas and furnished the house with the shipment that had arrived from Wloclawek.

When we went to have tea with the aunts, Lev carried Alionushka in his arms. She wore a hat that covered her ears, and red mittens. In the aunts' living room it was warm and cosy.

Having a meal at an inn on our way back to Wloclawek,
and listening to an old harpist playing traditional Polish airs

Tea with the aunts. Bread is being toasted on the grate and the samovar is steaming away.

Grigory takes Lev's coat as he comes in out of the cold.

We were greeted on our arrival by Grigory, the elder of the menservants (there was another one named Feodor) and he took our coats. In the drawing room a samovar was boiling on a round table covered with a cloth. There was a cake, fresh brioches and buns with jam. In one corner a fire burned in the fireplace and Aunt Sasha poured the tea. Manya, one of Uncle Nicholas's three illegitimate daughers, took Alionushka on her lap and offered her a brioche, but she made a fuss and stretched her arms out to me.

Manya said that Uncle wanted to give us a cow. I flushed with pleasure. We drank tea. Everyone was gay and happy.

A T FIRST our modest, even poor, house seemed strange to us, but very quickly we grew accustomed to it and indeed came to like it precisely because of its modesty, which cancelled all materialistic considerations. It was evidence of a contempt for all that was petty and mean; and everything in Kamenka was so real and virtuous that its inhabitants, its servants and its guests, seemed to form an indestructible entity. The other Davydoffs, those of Yurchikha and Verbovka, had become civilized in the empty sense of the word; they had good beds and had arranged their houses in a modern way, according to what was in fashion, but Kamenka itself remained as Uncle Nicholas had found it in the first half of the nineteenth century.

Uncle Nicholas came to see our house. Striking the floor with his feet and his cane, he asked if I was pleased and apologized for the fact that everything was in such poor condition.

Everything seemed marvellous to us as winter set in. Lev earned 250 roubles a month plus our living expenses. We had hired a young girl named Dunya and had also brought a cook from Matussov by the name of Ivan Novokhatko, who reigned over a rather dark kitchen that was full of smoke.

My kitchen at Kamenka, in the charge of our chef, Ivan Novokhatko

Thick snow is falling now. In two days' time it will be Christmas Eve. There is a smell of snow and frost. The pine trees and the shrubs around the house are like blue porcelain. Today I will go to the woods with Lev to find a buck. We must have a good roast for the festivities.

After lunch, a "grinjal", a low sleigh with wider runners used to transport heavy goods in winter, is driven up in front of the porch of the big house. Lev and I sit down in it. Over my pelisse I put a "burka", a Caucasian felt coat, which belongs to Uncle Nicholas, and Lev wears his bearskin coat. The footmen stick pieces of fur in the corners to add warmth, and we are off! Alionushka looks through the window and claps her hands on the pane.

We pass below Yurchikha, then along undulating hills. Close to the Podlesnoe farm we climb up by a lane into peaceful white forest. From time to time a lump of snow falls from a branch and softly strikes us.

Lev has moved his legs out of the lambskins and has loaded his gun. We keep a look out for spoor on the fresh snow. Here are rabbit tracks and there are the small triangular markings of birds, and further on we see where a fox has passed. And now we hear a dull sound and in front of us a buck trots by. Lev trembles but does not raise his gun. Sidor, the coachman, has also reacted and smiles.

We glide on slowly, looking right and left, and suddenly Sidor pulls up the horses and points with his whip to the right. Lev jumps from the sleigh and hides behind a large oak tree. We move slowly forward; there, about forty paces ahead of us, stands a stag, its head with beautiful antlers raised high, following the horses with its eyes. A shot rings out and the beast makes two or three bounds forward before crashing to the ground.

I close my eyes. I hate hunting. I hold the reins while Sidor and Lev run to their prey and drag the stag by its hind legs to the sleigh.

"Let's go for a ride in the forest," says Lev. "It's still early."

Lev shooting a stag. I remain on the sleigh and our coachman Sidor holds the reins

ALREADY ON THE MORNING of Christmas Eve the fir tree has been brought into the dining room. We keep Alionushka in the drawing room so that she will not see us decorating it. Its scent spreads through the whole house and I set fire on purpose to a few small branches so that the smell of Christmas may be everywhere. The tree has been set in the corner near the window and its dark branches stand out against the snowy background.

I hang up golden nuts that I have been painting all week. The gold sparkles as if the nuts were alive. Here are the Crimean apples with their red cheeks; they hang heavily at the tip of the branches. We tie on tangerines. In Kamenka all the fruits, sweets, chocolate, anything can be found in the Jewish shops.

It is freezing, about -10°C! The aunts have arrived and are playing with Alionushka in the drawing room. Lev and I light the tree and open wide the doors that give on to the corridor. Alionushka enters, holding the hand of Sasha Novokhatko, the cook's son, and she looks wide-eyed at the tree, the miracle-tree. Behind her come the aunts, and then the nursemaid, Anna Nikolaevna, who is the daughter of the aunts' housekeeper.

Sasha looks at the tree without saying a word or smiling, while Alionushka claps her hands, whistles and covers him in paper wrappings.

CHRISTMAS ON THE ESTATE is an occasion of joy. The snow crackles under the shoes of the women and the children all dressed in their Sunday best. They stand by their men, their faces painted with ochre or black soot or simply with chalk, stuffing themselves with food and behaving naughtily while the sun sinks into the scarlet snow as if it were on fire.

Soon the meadows will empty, the fires will be lit in the *khatkas* – the Ukrainian peasant homes – and Christmas Eve will start with the ringing of the church bells calling the faithful to mass.

The decorated Christmas tree in the aunts' dining room

Christmas dinner: Uncle Nicholas, the aunts, Lev, Alionushka and I

The aunts going off to mass on Christmas Eve

CHRISTMAS WAS FOR ME the best time of the year, the most intimate, the cosiest, especially that first year in Kamenka when the revolution was spreading and the whole of Russia was erupting with riots, strikes and demonstrations.

At that time there lived in Kamenka a notary, a certain Dolenga-Semenovsky, a very able, decided, intelligent and energetic man, in spite of his unprepossessing looks. He had a hard face with large, cruel and searching eyes. He spoke in a manner that brooked no discussion.

One day when he was chatting with Lev, Dolenga-Semenovsky asked, "Who is Nicholas Vassilyevich's heir?" Lev answered that for the time being nothing had been decided, and he told him the story of the exiled Decembrist grandfather, the fact that only the children born

Uncle Nicholas and the notary Dolenga-Semenovsky discussing Uncle's will

after the marriage of their parents before the exile were entitled to an inheritance, that is, Pyotr and Nicholas. If the latter did not make a will, the sole legal heirs would be the three brothers in Yurchikha. Dolenga said, "Oh no! The inheritance should be yours because you work here and are so close to him."

Lev did not believe Uncle Nicholas would ever bring himself to do that. But the fiery Dolenga-Semenovsky was determined to persuade him. Uncle Nicholas hummed and hawed: "Yes, I wanted to leave everything to my brother Alexey but he died . . ."

"You must do something because the people at Yurchikha are dangerous," said Dolenga, getting very excited and using colourful language.

A little while later he came back to the subject but Uncle Nicholas could only answer, "I have done nothing but think about it."

"You should leave everything to Lev Alexeyevich," insisted Dolenga. "You like him and he will not abandon Kamenka, he will not offend anyone, and he will continue to live here as you have done."

And so it came about, in early February 1906, that Uncle Nicholas signed a will in favour of Lev Alexeyevich Davydoff.

THE EVENING AFTER Dolenga brought us the news about Uncle Nicholas's will, we could not sleep for ages. Lev was almost stunned, but gathered up his courage to keep from showing anything because Uncle Nicholas had asked that no one be told.

Our household was blossoming. We had a first-class cook in Novokhatko. I myself took care of the dairy products. I prepared a wonderful fresh cream which people would come and regale themselves on. One day at the market Lev bought me a pedigree pig, a sow with an upturned nose, for 25 roubles. I called it Matriochka. We loved to walk through the market. It started next to our fence, to which the muzhiks would tie their carts and stalls. The Jewish shops swarmed with people. Crowds filled the street where Jewish vendors sold horses and calves.

February ends and March is here. The months, with their change of weather suddenly breaking the rhythm of our life, start to whisper in our ears, "Spring! Spring!" The days grow longer, the sun shines through the windows and warms our rooms. The larks start to sing, the snow has melted in the fields, the sowers have begun their work on the still wet soil and are followed by the harrows. On March 9th we go out in a drozhky in spite of the mud, to see how the sowing is proceeding. It is warm in the carriage which Sidor drives as in winter.

When we return home, boiling tea is awaiting us near the fireplace in the aunts' house, and we warm our frozen hands by the fire while we tell them what we have been doing.

In early spring Lev and I go out in a drozhky to watch the sowing

HOLY WEEK IS FILLED with all sorts of events. People hasten to the church while in the kitchen and bakeries the Easter cakes and brioches are rising. Housewives kneeling piously for the service think, "Oh, I haven't yet strained the white cheese for the paskha!"

On Thursday people get busy in the larder, the bakery and the kitchen. Pounds and pounds of flour are spread on the boards, on tables and in basins. Hundreds of eggs are broken. Sugar is poured without being measured. Almonds, raisins, saffron, nutmeg are added.

With Alionushka I gaze at all this and delightedly breathe the fragrant fumes, because today we fast, and everywhere in the house and in the courtyard there is the smell of sunflower oil . . . We go with the housekeeper to the larder, where she shows us the paskhas and the painted eggs that have been prepared for the servants. Alionushka jumps on the weighing machine and swings herself.

Preparations for Easter. Alionushka and I with the housekeeper in the larder.
Each servant will receive one paskha and a dozen painted eggs

THE DAY BEFORE EASTER, on Passion Sunday, at 9 a.m. in the big house, after a short grace at the buffet, a priest blessed the paskhas that the servant brought in, and for the first time sang "Kristos Voskresse!" (Christ is risen!) Aunt Sasha, who fasted during the whole of Lent, raised her face adoringly towards the priest and a great joy shone in her eyes.

After blessing the Easter fare, Father Dimitry removed his mitre and paid his respects to the aunts, inviting them to go to church for the Easter service.

All who were able to go put on white dresses, and the children stuck flowers and a mass of ribbons in their hair. The little country church became alive with the gay chatter of people. Though it was barely 100 feet from our house, we always took the coach to go there. It was all lit up, and in the still moist grass around it oil lamps burned with bright and smoky flames. We remained standing throughout the service but returned home before mass. There awaiting us were the traditional coffee and paskha, cake and the rest of the Easter fare.

Father Dimitry blessing the Easter table

SPRING ADVANCES by rapid stages. Every day in every farm, things are moving and progressing. Temporary workers are hired, cattle are inventoried, the worthless animals are eliminated. Everyone is busy in the office. Here are the two stewards, all red from the wind. The old gamekeeper is there too, as well as the old manager of the sugar factory. They are all there standing around Uncle Nicholas and Lev.

Alionushka, Anna Nikolaevna and I go for a walk in the garden, still wearing our winter coats, and pick crocuses, those dark lilac-coloured flowers, the first to bloom after the snow melts. How they smell of honey! After them, small blue asters break out in masses all along the fence through the old leaves under the trees, and when the sun becomes warmer it will be the turn of the pale violets way down at the bottom of the garden.

What delight! The garden covered 10–15 *dessiatines*, almost all on a slope that dropped down to the Tiasmin river. I have never seen so many flowering lilac trees anywhere else. There were simple ones, pedigree, mossy, Persian ones, pink ones, every sort one could imagine. In early April we would walk as if bewitched by this mass of colours, which we never had enough of, especially if they had been dampened by a warm spring shower. We walked down moist lanes between lawns that were beginning to look green. We sat on a bench while Alionushka ran down the lanes with one of the dachshunds.

The lilacs in the large garden at Kamenka

THE SUMMER OF 1906 was a troubled one. Various rumours were circulated. At one moment, people said that a family of landowners had been locked into their country house and burnt alive by the muzhiks. Another time we heard that a steward's cottage had been burned down. When a fire was detected in the neighbourhood, the churches rang the tocsin. Sometimes we heard them ringing all night, close by or far away and all of us rushed to the fire to see how the wind was tearing away burning hay and blowing it over to the village, thus starting new fires.

Our turn came. One afternoon at 2 o'clock a horseman rode over from Podlesnoe to tell us that the farm was on fire. This was our first serious alarm. Lev and I rushed over to the stables which were on the other side of the road, seized the horses and sped to the scene of the fire. On the road we were overtaken by the intendant Varvashin, who was also on his way to Podlesnoe, so we jumped into his drozhky and went with him.

The long stable, flanked by stalls for eighty oxen, with a pigsty next to it and a larder – everything was on fire. It was obvious that, during the lunchtime break, someone had set fire to the side that overlooked the fields. The water hose was already in action; firemen from other villages arrived and helped to extinguish the fire. Lev and I ran among the embers and threw out those that were still burning. Thank God, none of the cattle had been burnt, and the damage was limited to the thatched roof. The brick walls had resisted.

Rushing to the fire at Podlesnoe

THE FIELDS WERE COVERED with almost ripe golden wheat. For a long time Lev and Varvashin had been discussing the harvesting with Uncle Nicholas, but a sort of malaise reigned in the office. Varvashin and the steward said that the peasants were demanding an extra sheaf and simply strolled around refusing to go to work, preferring to make trouble in the village and to act in a threatening manner. The men in the office didn't know what to do.

The first day of harvesting arrived, but no workmen appeared. On the second and third days, there were still no workers. The muzhiks said that they would start harvesting only if they were given what they had asked for. The state of tension having reached its peak, Lev asked his cousin Mitya to cable the governor for a detachment of dragoons.

Huge crowds assembled near the town hall (at that time Kamenka had around 8,500 inhabitants, two churches and two rural districts) and waited. The day came when the dragoons were supposed to arrive, and a group of us went out to greet them. Malevolent and treacherous faces stared at us as we walked through the village. In a little while a torrential rain fell on us with thunder and lightning. We remained standing stoically, drenched and dirtied by the mud, our hair hanging down our noses! Suddenly, from behind the rise, we saw arriving down the road the detachment of dragoons with an officer at their head, all singing a marching song. We shouted enthusiastically, and when the smart soldiers in their white shirts passed in front of us, we hugged the necks of their horses.

The wheat was ripe and had been flattened by the torrential rain, so it had to be harvested at all costs. That evening, when we had dinner with the aunts, everyone was calm. Uncle didn't even mention the events that were taking place.

On our way home in the dark night, we found everything silent and empty. Tonight we could sleep peacefully: the dragoons were keeping watch. But in the middle of the night I was suddenly wakened by the ringing of the tocsin in both churches. From far off we could hear faintly the sounds of rioting, voices, the stamping of a horse's hoofs. Quickly the sounds came closer and a horseman was slapping at our door with his whip. "I have come to fetch Lev Alexeyevich!" he shouted. "The Nikolaevsky farm is on fire!" Lev seemed to dress in a matter of seconds and dashed from the house.

It was not until morning that he returned and described the ugly situation that had developed between the dragoons and the peasants. The commanding officer of the detachment had ordered that the instigators of the fire be brought to him; when there was no response to this, he had decided to requisition the peasants – that is, to feed his men and

The arrival of the dragoons

horses at their expense. Soldiers had therefore been despatched to the villages to take all they could lay their hands on – cattle, bread, grain, milk, butter.

We were extremely worried and Lev went over to see the officer in charge to ask him to put an end to this affair. He argued that relations with the peasants were already very difficult and that such a measure could only make matters worse. Nevertheless, it continued until evening and only ended the following morning, when the stewards and the authorities went to call the men to work at 4 a.m., saying they could have the extra sheaf.

The dragoons stayed a few more days, then left when the fields were filled with people, as in more peaceful times. We were sorry to see them go, and also a little afraid.

THE DISAGREEMENT having been settled, the gathering of the wheat has begun. We walk around the farms and admire how each day the haystacks grow on the large fields. The sun is warm. It is early July. The peasants have started taking the third sheaf. Their stacks rise as high as houses.

It is almost noon and the women have already stopped work. One is feeding her newborn baby. Another is sleeping peacefully under a tent made of rags tied to three posts to protect her from the sun.

After gazing at all this, we return home in a cabriolet driven by Lev. At home borscht awaits us, with pork, tomatoes, kasha, delicious fresh kvass, roast chicken and ice cream.

The harvesting of the wheat

THE SUN GOES DOWN. A purple light sets the horizon aflame. There is not a cloud in the sky. In the afternoon the temperature has risen to 26°C in the shade. No one has ventured out of the house before 5 but now everyone is outside. The young women gardeners hitch up their skirts above their knees and water the plants abundantly with water taken from the barrels where it has warmed up all day. Ivan, uncle's gardener, supervises the work. He is a bald, not very tall man with a sly expression. He has six young assistants who, in the evening, water the plants that wilt under the stifling heat. Ivan attaches a great deal of importance to the flower beds and always makes a point of being present when they are watered.

At sunset I take Alionushka to the aunts' house and play with her in the small garden, breathing that wonderful atmosphere of wet grass. Soon Anna Nikolaevna takes away my little girl for her nap while we remain with the aunts on the terrace. Glass candlesticks stand on the table and the whole household arrives: Sasha, Vera, Nina, Katya, Shura, Manya, Varya, Minya Romanovna, Verochka who has just finished the Institute, and her brother Kolya Sandberg who is a student. The young ones are discreetly silent. Uncle chats with Lev. We have meat cutlets with a raisin sauce, and rice pudding with fresh cream. The samovar boils at one end of the table and Aunt Sasha pours tea into drinking glasses.

Turning to me she says: "Our food must not seem very good to you. I hear you have a good cook," and she laughs guiltily.

Indeed their cook, Jacob, is as old as he is bad. He prepares what he likes and in whatever way he feels like doing it. Usually for lunch he prepares a soup, a very light, liquid soup. It would be all right if it were borscht but it is only a liquid bouillon, which is strange because he is allotted one pound of meat per person, rice and vermicelli. This is followed by roast chicken or by a lean fillet that is rather old and bloodless, with spinach or peas. Dessert consists of cake, jelly or blancmange, several types of preserves, and in summer a fruit macedoine in a watermelon. Fortunately the products are fresh because Jacob is anything but a chef and has no culinary talent whatsoever . . .

100

Uncle Nicholas's garden in the heat of summer

The opening of the hunting season in September

THE OPENING of the hunting season took place in September. It was Yuri, who lived with Uncle Nicholas's permission in a smallholding next to the Big Wood, that usually organized the hunts, but this year Lev has taken over. He has invited the neighbours, and early one morning, Lev's brother Grisha and our cousin Kolya Sandberg go to the meeting place in the forest. The ladies meet them at twelve for lunch.

The hunting season signifies the beginning of a new era for the village. It marks the end of agricultural activities, the end of summer and the prospect of the unique autumn of Little Russia.

It is still very warm in the first half of September, but the light has already changed. At 10 a.m. the carriage appears which will convey the lunch, the samovar, the cooks and the servants to the forest clearing. We follow at 11, in summer dresses with scarves around our heads, a fashion I have introduced in place of town hats.

The meeting place is a clearing with fresh green grass that has grown after the dry spell in the autumnal dampness. The horses are unharnessed and start grazing right away. A barrel of water is installed and the carriages are placed in the shade. In the centre of the clearing the hunters' table is set up with mounds of straw around it for seats.

The carriages with the hunters arrive, their rifles smelling of powder. Lev shouts, "Grigory, bring the glasses!" Everyone moves towards the table, vodka flows, glasses clink. Grigory hurriedly brings the zakusky, and the famished hunters grab at them while the dead animals are taken out of the carriages and lined up on the ground. The lunch menu is always the same: zakusky, vodka, borscht with pirozhky, mutton or another meat stew, biscuits, fruit and of course several sorts of wine.

AUTUMN ARRIVED, and even though the days were still warm we sealed up the windows and doors to keep the cold out of the house. Manya already muffled herself up in shawls. Her nose had gone red and her lips were dry and cracked.

Poor Manya had been convinced after many years to go and see her unmarried mother, who lived quietly in the village. She continued to see her occasionally, and when the woman died, she was buried in the church cemetery. From then on Manya visited the grave regularly. Manya had made a good and kind gesture towards her mother, particularly as they did not meet on the same footing, Manya having been brought up in gentility and her mother a servant.

Cold weather returns. Manya, who particularly feels the cold, is huddled in shawls.
Aunt Lisa wears an eyeshade because she is sensitive to light

THE RAINS HAVE STARTED and there is frost in the morning. The village is all dark and only the shop windows throw a pale light outside as the doors are tightly closed.

Small low Jewish shops line both sides of the long paved street that divides the village in two. The Jews sell everything – wool, cotton, material of all sorts, cheviot, taffeta, moiré, as well as haberdashery, wine, fruits. The inhabitants of Kamenka and the neighbouring villages, the landowners and the workers on the estate, all go to the Jewish shops. They can find saddles, rope, soap, perfume, pencils, crockery, suet, nails, barrels of oil, furniture, kerosene, candles, light bulbs – anything you care to name.

If you walked into a fabric shop, three or four attendants would pounce on you, and you couldn't possibly leave without their showing you everything that was in the shop. "You don't need to show me all that," we would say, "we haven't come for that today."

"Sit down, please," the owner would say, pushing forward a chair. "It is only to show you. You don't need to buy."

"All I want is some nainsook," I would say, and he answered, "We have some. Of course we have some. But look at this!" He unrolled a marvellous dark blue woollen cloth. "It has just arrived. Take it for a dress. You will be delighted with it."

"It is very nice, but today I only want some nainsook."

"What about this?" and he would throw a bright green Liberty print onto the counter. "But nainsook . . . ?"

"Yes, yes, here is some nainsook. Moshe! Cut one arshin of nainsook!" And while Moshe cuts the nainsook, the sales talk goes on and on.

The Jewish fabric shop in Kamenka village

THE BIG FAIR in Zlatopol took place during October. Zlatopol was a large village, much larger than Kamenka. Each year we needed horses and oxen for the estate. Lev and I decided to go there with Sarancha, our experienced manager, to learn how to buy and not to be cheated.

We rode into Zlatopol at noon. The enormous square was completely occupied by the fair. We edged our way through the carts and the cattle, and stopped near the centre. Sarancha descended from our cart and disappeared. The gypsies and the Jews were running in every direction and showing off their horses. A muzhik slapped a Jew's hand after haggling over a horse.

After a lunch of pirozhky, salami and wine, we went nosing around. What noise! What commotion! We ran into an argument between two gypsies and had no notion what it was all about.

One shouted to Lev, "Here, hold these horses for me! I was just saying to him – "

People were trying to move me away from Lev, who was saying, "But I don't want your old nags!"

The others started shouting even louder while pinning us more and more. Lev was reaching into his pocket for some money; the gypsies became more agitated, and another one joined in.

"Just lend me 100 roubles for one minute! I only want to hold it in my hand!"

"Don't give it to him! He's a crook!"

I was gripped by such a feeling of terror that I grabbed Lev's sleeve and tugged to get him away from there. I was certain this was all a trap, a comedy acted out to rob us. Sarancha knew all these tricks and had tried several times to extricate us, but the people, all of them brigands, prevented him. We finally got away with difficulty, and the whole band dispersed at once.

Sarancha managed to buy a pair of oxen. Together we bought a dozen horses two hours later, and after tying their bridles to our cart we set off for home.

Lev and I among the crowd at the fair in Zlatopol

WINTER AGAIN! I don't know how the others felt, but as for me, my heart thumped and my soul trembled when I thought of snow. Of course the winter was long and often harsh. For people who lived in poor northern villages far from any railway, buried under masses of snow in primitive homes miles away from all other people, six or seven months of winter were not easy to endure. But in Kamenka, only 2 versts by paved road from the railway, living on a lovely estate among neighbours, and Kiev within easy reach, it was quite another matter.

On a day when everything is covered in snow, we go to the Podlesnoe farm which we love so much. New roofs have been built since the fire, and even the small barns are ready. It is a pleasure to see how the buildings have improved.

Podlesnoe farm in the winter

77

AT 4 P.M. IT IS TIME to go home. As the horses trot off joyfully, snow begins to fall. It crackles under the runners of our sleigh. White frost covers Lev's moustache and beard. The road passes alongside a frozen pond, and here are the first houses of Yurchikha. The snow-covered horses slow down to a walk, but the snow falls even harder. When we leave Yurchikha, the wind catches us and raises snow from the fields, dry as sand. We can't see anything; the horizon is invisible behind the milky haze.

"Where are we?" Lev asks Sidor. "You've turned around."

"No, I am on the right road," Sidor answers.

"We are in a field!" I shout, and a strange anxiety grips us as we realize we have lost our way. No trace of a road can be seen or heard under the horses' hoofs.

Sidor finally admits that he has lost his way, but he is confident the horses will take us home.

Suddenly something dark passes in front of us. Sidor cries out, "Hey! Is this the road to Kamenka?"

"Yes," answers a muffled voice.

"Right or left?"

"Left for Kamenka," and the ghostly presence vanishes.

A quarter of an hour later we see the dark grey houses of our village.

THE BLIZZARD continued all night, covering the balcony and the windows with snow. In the morning we woke to the sound of shovels digging us out. In every house stoves crackled and were heated to the maximum. The winter scents of burning and smoke were everywhere.

Alionushka was already dressed and climbed on the window sill. We both admired the view from there. What a fall of snow there had been! Blue trenches ran through the immaculate whiteness under the shovel of Bolitsky and the other workmen.

Lost in the snow

79

Digging out after the blizzard

I ASKED FOR the snow to be swept off a large section of the pond below the garden, and I went ice-skating there every day. Alionushka came to slide on the ice and ride in a sleigh. On the other side of the pond one could see the smoke and hear the noise of our sugar factory and even smell the pressed beets. On the bridge over the Tiasmin passed long files of ox-drawn carts carrying the pressed beets from the Nikolaevsky farm and horse-drawn carts taking away the bales of sugar from the courtyard.

ONE OF THE WINTER pastimes I invented was to ride in a sleigh drawn by dogs. Manya had a collie named Orlik which had had two little bitches by a curly-haired mongrel. These two large and hairy beasts, Lissa and Latochka, were therefore half pedigreed. I had the idea of harnessing them to a light sleigh that I had bought. On calm winter days Tolya, the twelve-year-old son of Anna Feodorovna, Alionushka and I would go riding and, in order to make the bitches run (they had never been trained), we tied pieces of meat on the end of a long whip and they would try to catch them, running as fast as they could, thus conveying us at top speed along the snow-packed alleys.

Skating on the pond at the bottom of the garden

de with Alionushka's ponies

119

Riding in a sleigh drawn by two dogs

1906 – Christmas at the Donats'

EDWARD FEODOROVICH DONAT started his career in Kamenka as a young and well-educated trainee. He came from an excellent family, not Germans but rather Germanized Balts. At university he studied agronomy, and before graduating he had to undertake a practical training course. It was then that he became steward at Podlesnoe. He married a charming young girl, Lydia Anatolyevna, from his social set, and was promoted to the post of manager. After spending a few years in Kamenka, he became the manager of Gruchevsk, a nearby estate owned by relatives called Bobrinsky, but he remained on friendly terms with Kamenka. Once upon a time Gruchevsk had belonged to the Davydoffs, but one of the Decembrist's brothers, a notorious gambler, had lost it to his neighbour Bobrinsky.

The Donats' home was gay and hospitable, always filled with charming young people. In 1906 we spent Christmas with them. Their two lovely daughters and a number of cousins delighted us all with dancing and games. It was that day that I heard for the first time, spoken by the young Donat cousins, new revolutionary expressions such as "arbitrary decisions", "the right to freedom of speech", that seemed out of place in this warm atmosphere of comfort and refinement.

DURING THE SUMMER of 1908, Volodya Krassovsky, one of Lev's former comrades-in-arms, came to visit us and complained about the way his estate in the province of Kherson was being mismanaged. He was in any case bored on his remote estate, and we suggested that he sell it and buy something in our neighbourhood. Close to Kamenka lived a widower who was no longer young and had grown-up sons. When he remarried a younger woman and had a son by her, he decided to sell his estate, Dubrova, in order to assure their financial future.

Krassovsky, Lev and I drove over to see the owner of Dubrova. No sooner had we driven into the forest than we were seized by a feeling of delight and charmed by the wonderful scents that emanated from it.

The house was not very large, only one storey high, and a bit pretentious-looking with urns on the roof and a terrace that gave onto the wood. The owner greeted us in a friendly fashion and showed us around the house, the farm and the park. I walked as if in a trance. Though I kept praising it to Krassovsky, I felt a terrible envy gnawing away at my heart, and I almost cried at the thought that we could not buy it ourselves.

Krassovsky was happy to buy it, but was not able to do so before selling his own estate. Lev offered to put up the deposit for him, and that was done not long after our visit. But the thought of Dubrova would not leave me in peace. I would say to Lev, "Why don't you buy it yourself? Does Krassovsky really need such a big estate? He is alone. He will not really live there!"

In January, when the deed of sale was to be signed, Krassovsky wrote to Lev to say that he had not been able to raise the money and had given up the idea of buying Dubrova. With tears in my eyes I begged Lev to buy it. He had to think it over in his logical and rational way. Money was required. He asked advice of those whose opinion he respected . . . Finally he reached the decision to borrow the money from Kamenka and buy Dubrova in my name! When he settled the whole thing he was beaming. "All is well," he said, "Dubrova is ours. You may settle there whenever you wish!"

DURING THAT 1908/09 WINTER we suddenly decided to go abroad. We had not left Kamenka for three years. Uncle Nicholas was his usual kind self when he gave his blessing to our trip to Nice.

It was an interesting journey. There were snowstorms in Italy, so strong that we reached Genoa only with great difficulty and nine hours late. We had to stop there because the train went no further.

After a bad night in Genoa, we went on to Nice, where the weather was clear and warm, the air fragrant with the scent of flowers. We stayed at the Hotel Splendide on the rue Victor Hugo, where we had large rooms, light and warm.

Two months in Nice did wonders for my health and spirits.

ON THE WAY HOME from Nice, we stopped off in Brittany to see my sister Juliet and her husband Georges Courtin. After all the sun and heat of the Riviera, Moros, the château where they lived near Concarneau, seemed damp and ugly with its humid rooms, its icy cold sheets and the continuous rain.

But we were homesick by now and my heart grew lighter as we started on the long journey back to Kamenka. On the final lap, there was rain turning to hail, then snow. Where was the sun of Nice? Something warmer than the Riviera sun filled my heart as I saw the Pliakovsky stream. The train began to brake down the hill side. We were ready, standing by the exit. When the train stopped, we could see the stationmaster on the platform with his red cap and his collar turned up; and the servants were all turning their backs to the wind.

We hurled ourselves out of the carriage. Grigory and the groom were there with the horse cart for the luggage. We were caught by the storm and I threw myself at Alionushka and wrapped her up in my plaid.

After a wild drive through the snow, we stopped at the aunts' house to have a cup of coffee with them. Aunt Sasha, Aunt Lisa, Aunt Katya and Aunt Vera were all standing at the windows. On the porch we were grabbed again by the snowstorm, but in the hallway it was warm, the stoves were going full blast.

We were home again.

Our departure in the snow for Nice

3 Dubrova, War and Revolution

IT WAS NOT till the end of April that we moved to Dubrova. We took the entire staff with us. We bought a cow, and all the food was brought from Kamenka.

A young soldier, highly recommended, was named steward. He was first sent to the Nikolaevsky farm to learn the job, but he created such a good impression right from the start that Lev had no hesitation in naming him steward of Dubrova. He came from Moldavia and was a very handsome man. His name was Yaposkurt.

The animals were in poor condition and we set at once to renew the stock. We inspected our new possessions on a hot May day, and not the smallest spot went unexamined. The trough for the cattle near the well, the large enclosures, the barns, the servants' quarters, everything was wonderful.

There was an 80-*dessiatine* park separated by a ditch from our land on one side, and on the other from that of our neighbours, the Rogovskis, who were Polish. I loved to sit on the edge of that ditch and look in the distance at what seemed to be blue sea. That particular spot was called "the three oak trees", because three very thick oak trees grew there, covered by large stag beetles.

We put everything we had into Dubrova, all our hearts, our tastes and our creative spirit.

SOON AFTER WE MOVED to Dubrova we got to know a charming family called Szymanowski, who owned a small estate Tymoshovka not far from Verbovka. The Szymanowskis had two sons, Felix, who was a pianist, and Karol, a composer, and there were three daughters. Their house was large, with a garden that sloped down gently towards a pond.

Sometimes when we visited them, only a small group of neighbours were there, and then Karol or Felix would sit at the piano and offer us sublime moments which I will never forget.

The "three oak trees" at Dubrova

A musical evening at the Szymanowskis'

The "uninitiated" went to the billiard room and played there, while in the semi-darkness of the drawing room, lit by only one kerosene lamp, we listened in rapt silence. Through one of the open windows we could see under the starry sky the dark outline of the pine trees that grew right next to the house, and through another, small flowering heads and lazy Glories of Dijon that climbed up the side of the house. Felix became another person when he sat at the piano and played a moving and tortured Chopin *Ballade* or Schumann's *Carnaval*. As for Karol, he seemed to become immaterial as his beautiful hands moved over the keyboard creating sounds that were not of this earth.

It was only when the "uninitiated" returned to the drawing room and announced that the horses were ready, that one's dream was shattered.

OUR SECOND SUMMER at Dubrova was a particularly hot one. At the end of the day, as evening started to fall, we would get ready to go somewhere, for instance to pick flowers or gather mushrooms in the forest, but one time we decided to fish for freshwater crayfish in the pond. The evening was bewitching, and I ordered the coach to be harnessed as well as the cart for our cook Ivan, because we had decided to eat out in the open air.

We settled ourselves near the pond, tied small pieces of meat at the end of lines and plunged them into the water. Very soon we caught enormous crayfish that lived on the sandy bottom. We had taken with us Aniuta, our clever and resourceful chambermaid, who stepped into the water naked and caught crayfish with her hands after searching for them on the muddy bottom. Alexander Mikhailovich Boborikin, the notary who had handled the Dubrova deed of sale, sat close to the edge of the pond, on a small folding stool, and gazed with delight at her fishing and even more at the graceful shape of Aniuta's breasts, which would pop every minute in and out of the water as she lifted her hand holding a crayfish.

A bonfire had been lit on the embankment and its flames rose lively and gay, their reflection in the water resembling red serpents. The cook had started to prepare the first pot of water and he set it on the fire while Alionushka delightedly threw raw potatoes on the hot embers.

We dined sitting on the thick grass and ate the fat crayfish with a ravenous appetite. We returned home in the clear night, gliding silently over the fields under the moon that lit up the whole steppe with its silvery rays that made the yellowing wheat shine and sparkle.

Fishing for crayfish in our pond

For the winter of 1909/10 we decided not to go abroad. Instead we left our pleasant Dubrova in September and moved to Kamenka. Of course, after Dubrova the house in Kamenka seemed wretched and we felt very cramped, although we were able to go to the annexes and the buildings attached to the house through our own corridor. But the stables and pigsties were only two steps away and naturally lacking in charm; also, Dubrova had spoiled us for the proximity of other houses and dirty village streets.

We made up our minds to spend Christmas in Dubrova, where we could have a Christmas tree for the children of the staff and for Alionushka. On Christmas Eve the children arrived, and the rest of the staff, about fifteen in all, grey with uncombed hair and wearing miserable old rags. They uttered not a word and showed no sign of joy or pleasure. We had prepared presents for them and Alionushka started to distribute them. They took them without a word, not really knowing quite what it all meant. An embarrassing silence reigned in the room. No one joined in Alionushka's joyous excitement, and they finally left as they had come.

During that winter we had no luck when we went stag-hunting. We never succeeded in getting close enough, even though we saw quite a few fine animals. We were driving back disappointed along the border of the Yurchikha forest, when we suddenly heard the barking of dogs in pursuit of prey. We stopped and our driver Tadeus looked back. "Sir," he said, "those dogs are chasing a stag." But a few moments later the barking stopped. All at once a beautiful hunting dog appeared and stopped when it saw us. There were many stray dogs that fed on wild game and orders had been given to shoot them without pity. Delighted at a reason for loading his gun and furious that strange dogs should be hunting in our woods — not to speak of his dissatisfaction at having failed to shoot a stag — Lev raised his gun and aimed at the motionless animal.

I barely had time to shout, "Lev, don't shoot it! It may be Vassya's dog!" as the shot was fired. The dog didn't budge. Then, having lowered its head as if searching for game, it ran off in the direction of the Yurchikha wood and disappeared. I made the sign of the cross: "Thank God you missed him! If you hadn't, there'd have been a terrible row!"

As we started for home we had moved only a few steps when we came upon a beautiful stag and Lev shot him. Tadeus got down and tied him onto the sleigh at our feet, and we drove home very pleased with ourselves.

But it turned out that the dog had indeed been shot, that it was found dead two days later, and that it was Vassya's best hunting dog. To our astonishment, this led to a court hearing which proved to be so ludicrous that Lev and Vassya made it up and there were no hard feelings.

*Tadeus shooting at the stray dogs that preyed on game
and other animals near the Kamenka slaughterhouse.*

135

The comfortable office we arranged for Lev in the aunts' house

For some time we had felt that there was something amiss in the way the Kamenka houses were shared out, particularly as regarded the big house and ours, which were run on the same budget. It seemed more logical to have everyone in the same house. Furthermore, there was a lack of housing for the employees. In the large house, despite all Manya's efforts, conditions were primitive. Uncle Nicholas, with his generous nature, did not look into domestic details and simply supported Lev's decisions, even when these were important ones. Once again he entirely approved of the project. "Mariamna knows how to do this. Of course it will be better for you and much easier if you move in with my sisters," he agreed.

Without thinking any more about it, we announced that we were moving into the big house. Our servants, our furniture, our cattle and ourselves, everything was moved there. I also took my own housekeeper, which meant that the old one, Anna Feodorovna, had to be dismissed. The aunts' cook Jacob also went, which helped our diet enormously.

No exterior improvement could be started before springtime, but indoors we started making changes right away. The oak panel that had been in our dining room we moved to Lev's office, and fixed it up attractively with a game of chess on each side and a large writing table. With its claret-coloured walls, the office was very cosy. A lovely red carpet was laid on the floor and curtains hung on the windows.

We loved Lev's office and often stayed there warming ourselves at the fire in the corner.

IN THAT PERIOD before the 1914 War, the way people managed their land was undergoing many changes. I can only speak directly of our own circle, of the city of Kiev and its province, of Kherson and Chernigov, but I believe the same things were happening elsewhere.

Previously the landowners' wives had lived in their estates like reigning princesses, which in some ways they were. They never took any interest in household details; it was even considered improper for them to go into the kitchen or to look into the matter of provisions. Their housekeepers were there for that purpose, and they were given a free hand. My mother had been an exception. She was always deeply involved in the household chores and supervised everything – so that people would laugh, even a little scornfully, when they spoke about her.

My style was rather a different one. I wasn't interested like Mama in all aspects of the household, but I did study very carefully everything that had to do with the farm, and sent my poultry and livestock to shows.

As the general outlook changed, it became a matter of shame to ignore one's household. To behave like a retarded landowner's wife who never paid any attention to her enterprise and was totally devoid of all competence became disgraceful.

Once upon a time, literature and intellectual culture had been the privilege of the aristocratic class, but slowly they were beginning to reach other classes until, at the time I am speaking about, they had become universal. The same thing happened in agriculture. The peasants no longer threw the manure into the ditches but spread it on their fields. They started growing beets in an intensive way. The quality of their cattle improved because we sold them our pedigree calves. Soon interest in their farming enterprise grew.

THE NEXT CHRISTMAS, at Kamenka, winter was well installed and the traditional tree stood once more in the dining room, all decorated with gold trimmings, nuts, tangerines . . . and joy! Aunt Sasha went to church on Christmas Eve with her maid. It was a clear and snow-white evening and the temperature was -3° or -4°C. Christmas carollers ran around the courtyard with a star, peering through the windows and waiting for the moment when they would be let into the house to blare out "The Nativity of our Lord God." At 5 the tree was lit as it was done every year, with only the aunts present and Alionushka putting paper hats on their heads. Aunt Vera sat at the piano and played "Home Sweet Home", and we held each other's hands and danced around the tree singing. Lev returned from the factory emanating heat and the smell of beets.

The New Year! We eat, drink and make wishes! In the morning we are still in bed when the chambermaid Efimy and the housekeeper Anastasia Petrovna, wearing aprons filled with seeds, arrive in our room and throw them on us by the handful while murmuring, "Happy New Year! All best wishes of happiness! May God give a good harvest!" What an adorable custom!

Aunt Sasha going to church on Christmas Eve with her maid

1910. Кузьма Сокольник   M. Davidoff

Carollers with a Christmas star in the courtyard at Kamenka

THE WINTER of 1913/14 we spent in Kiev in an apartment we had found there the year before. It was a large, fourteen-room apartment with a little garden that required a great deal of redecorating and repair. I took many pieces of furniture from Matussov, among other things an old red divan that I put in the second hallway. When all the furniture had arrived and all the repairs had been done – this was in November – I went to Kiev for the finishing touches. I ordered the wallpaper and carpets and decided on our living arrangements. The governesses would live in the two rooms on the top floor, and next to them would be Alionushka's bedroom and classroom.

When the others arrived, Lev, Alionushka and all the servants who had not come with me, everything was in place, there were flowers everywhere, the fires were lit and coffee was ready in the dining room. The furniture in this pretty dining room had all been designed by my father for Matussov, and he himself had sculpted the frieze above the fireplace in 1886.

Every time I returned to Kamenka I visited Uncle Nicholas, who no longer felt strong enough to go to the big house in the evening for dinner. At dinner with his daughters and Dr. Zamyatin, who came to see him every day, he felt he was among his own people. I liked to go there. Everything was so decent and respectful, so simple and quiet.

That summer of 1914, we were gradually made aware of the news from Sarajevo. It became real to us when we saw the first class railway carriages full of officers at Kamenka station. Mobilization was at hand. The reservists were leaving and their wives accompanied them to the station. Two days later Lev was also called to Kiev; he was given the duty of preparing the reserve infantry regiment stationed at Akhturk, which displeased him intensely. When I heard about this I went to join him in Kiev.

After accompanying Lev to his train for Akhturk I returned to Kamenka. I went to see Aunt Sasha, then Uncle, to tell them all I had seen. "So now, Mariamna, you are all alone," said Uncle.

"I will take care of the whole concern," I answered, "and I will do it as best I know and as best I can."

In 1914 and 1915 Uncle Nicholas hardly went out of his house any longer, and on 2 April 1916 he died in bed at the age of 89.

The apartment we rented in Kiev during the winter of 1913–14

My bedroom in Kiev

HOW MANY INCIDENTS we lived through during the first years of the war in our Kiev apartment, especially in the drawing room. It was a warm and cosy room that lent itself to receptions, but I disliked those parties, and preferred to the provincial snobs the flock of cousins who arrived like little birds for tea at 5.

My bedroom was next to the drawing room. It was a very large room where I had assembled some antique furniture, placed all my trinkets, ordered a made-to-measure bed and hung up my favourite pictures and drawings. One day I drove to Matussov, which we had sold in 1915, and took a lot of the icons that hung on the walls there. I hung all these holy pictures over my bed and in the corner an icon that represented the golden head of Our Saviour, which had belonged to grandfather Vassily Lvovich Davydoff, the Decembrist, who had kept it during his whole exile.

After the important Brussels attack, all seemed calm at the Front. But then disquieting rumours started to circulate. Something seemed to be paralyzing the whole war effort. Yet these events did not affect our personal lives. We were sometimes as many as fifteen at the table for breakfast, and frequently after it I would go into town in our old Mercedes and would only get back home at about 4, when I would find the round table in the drawing room already set for tea and Zossim would bring in the samovar. A sofa stood near the table close to the stove, and I would sit there with my back to the wall, warming myself contentedly as the winter was dark and icy cold.

Early in March, or rather at the end of February, events which we had been expecting for a long time finally materialized. Alionushka had a tutor named Elisaveta Petrovna who had very leftist opinions. One day she was called to the phone and someone said to her, "There is a revolution in Petrograd!"

Several days went by in an atmosphere of excitement and enthusiasm. All my acquaintances were delighted by the turn of events – especially the abdication of the Tsar, that weakling. Maybe now the war would come to an end. But then we learned that the bolsheviks had taken control.

When we went to Kamenka everything seemed unchanged. Aunt Sasha greeted us. Grigory brought coffee and all the servants came to pay their respects. Their faces looked the same, as if there had been no revolution.

I often went there because each day brought something new. My farming enterprise, especially the cattle, was under the watchful eye of a very capable Swede, who made butter and wonderful cheeses. One day I went to the cowshed and took out a pure-bred Swiss cow which I led across the road to the big garden. She was a real beauty, all clean and washed,

Alionushka and I in the Kiev apartment at the time when the Revolution began.
Zossim, from the old days at Matussov, is serving us tea

Kamenka: our coachman Sidor wants to know who will be getting this cow

and I was very proud of her as I led her along and stopped in a little clearing where there was tall grass. She pounced on this delicacy and the juicy grass squeaked under her tongue.

"Here I am," I said to myself, "acting like a simple peasant. I brought her here myself to pasture without being afraid. I even made her cross the road to Kamenno."

Suddenly the voice of the coachman Sidor interrupted my thoughts. He came up to me and, looking at me with piercing eyes, his face all freckled over a red beard, said: "Who will this cow go to when the cattle are shared out?"

This question struck me like a whip. I didn't answer at once but finally, trying to hide my agitation, I said something simple and natural. "They will belong to whoever the provisional government will designate."

148

A FEW DAYS LATER we went to Verbovka. Yes, Verbovka had also changed. Elisaveta Petrovna reigned there with her hysterical socialist ideas. After tea, Lev's cousin Natasha and I went with her for a walk in the fields. As we gazed at the tender and smiling evening, it was as if all the agitation, the anxiety, the sorrow, existed only in our souls and nature did not share in our emotions. We walked on a well-trodden narrow road that passed through the wheatfields, and the ears of wheat rustled and caressed our faces. I asked Natasha if she thought this land would really go to the peasants. Instead of answering me, she threw a questioning glance at Elisaveta Petrovna, who said, "Of course."

"What are they going to do with this vast amount of land?" I asked.

"The same as you did," she answered with an arrogant look.

"That is quite impossible," I said, feeling that I was starting to boil inside. "They know nothing about the land, and in any case can you just take land from one person and give it to another? Can't they buy it, as they did when serfdom was abolished?"

"Not at all," she almost shouted. "You took it from the peasants so you must give it back to them!"

THE EVENINGS in Verbovka were no longer enjoyable. Our only moment of relaxation was when the Szymanowskis came over from Tymoshovka and Felix played the piano while all the others sat on the terrace, staring at the pitch-black night and thinking sad thoughts.

IN AUGUST 1918 we decided to go to Kiev as soon as possible, but some business affairs delayed us and I didn't want to leave Lev. Excesses were being committed everywhere. For instance, in Tymoshovka, where all the women had left for Elisavetgrad while Felix and Karol remained to try and save anything they could, not a day passed without some muzhik or other arriving, saying he had been sent by the authorities, and forcing them to open the suitcases they had been packing. Poor Felix would be hauled to the rural district office and subjected to all sorts of humiliations.

Aunt Lisa, Aunt Katya and Uncle had all died. Only Aunt Sasha was left, close to her century. She was blind and deaf, and never left her room. She would remain seated, silently knitting "by heart". She knew nothing about the revolution, but felt that something was going on and prayed all the time for her relatives.

The evenings were terrible. We would lock ourselves in, and I personally checked all the windows and doors, and made the rounds of the house. We were scared in the silent house. Those pleasant hours we used to spend in the drawing room were a thing of the past. We were the only ones left.

One night the sugar warehouse was broken into and many sacks of sugar stolen before Lev and a few servants were able to scare away the thieves. The very next day we started packing to go to Kiev. We had to leave Aunt Sasha behind with two women who looked after her, because she was no longer able to leave her bed. Once we left, the houses were invaded by peasants, who began to ransack the estate in earnest. In late November Aunt Sasha finally died. By then the peasants had begun to take the furniture away on their carts and drove triumphantly through the village with all their stolen goods.

We were back again in Kiev in our marvellous apartment. How well I felt there! Everything was peaceful and quiet around us; it almost seemed as if nothing had happened. I invited the Szymanowskis to stay with us, and the evenings I spent with them in the terracotta drawing room were pervaded by a special atmosphere, with the curtains drawn, the lamps lit under yellow shades and huge vases of chrysanthemum on the tables. Felix would play the piano while I set in front of him a glass of marsala, saying, "You may only drink this after you have played the Chopin Ballade."

As refugees appeared, fleeing from the bolsheviks, we took in old friends. I gave up my bedroom and moved into a smaller room on the ground floor. A large window gave on to the garden, and when there was a heavy snowfall the trees were covered by a sort of cotton wool, the sight of which made our thoughts fly to the country.

Zossim bringing a lamp as evening falls

The long Russian winter: bullfinches and tits at the window, 4 in the afternoon

CHRISTMAS WE CELEBRATED as always, with a big tree in the dining room. But black clouds were accumulating on the political horizon. People said the bolsheviks were preparing to attack Little Russia, and therefore the Ukraine.

Early in January, there was serious bombardment, making it impossible to go out of doors. Guns could be heard all day long. The Ukrainians were on the defensive. It lasted fifteen days until one night when the noise suddenly stopped. The bolsheviks had entered Kiev.

From then on, fear never left us. People were taken hostage right on the street. Fortunately the reign of terror did not reach us because we lived in a distant section of Kiev, not one favoured by rich people and aristocrats.

We learned that everything had been removed from Kamenka. People were living in the various houses and had taken away the cattle.

After three weeks, the bolsheviks began leaving Kiev, and there were rumours that German troops were on the way. And indeed, in February, Petliura and his men arrived, marching into the city to the cheers of crowds. Order returned immediately, as German patrols appeared every evening. The Germans also invaded the southern provinces and occupied Kamenka, where they forced the locals to return everything they had taken. We got back our possessions and although we never returned to Kamenka, work resumed there.

When the first nice days arrived we decided to rent a villa in Odessa. Food was sent from Kamenka, as in olden times. After a separate peace had been signed with the Germans, our old cook Ivan returned and we also took along two maids, a manservant and a kitchen maid.

We returned to Kiev in the autumn, and in early December we were told that the muzhiks of Kamenka were planning to come to Kiev to see Lev and me and demand explanations about certain private accounts we had with them. Everyone knew the meaning of this kind of interview. Many landowners had been taken away in this fashion, to face outlandish accusations and even death.

After their defeat the Germans left everything and gave up any sort of control. They knew that they would be going away any moment. What action should we take? Lev looked totally downcast but did nothing. We should hide, but where? I decided to go and stay with the Krupinskys, who lived in a fifth-floor apartment on Institute Street in an area called "Lipki" that seemed safer than ours. Lev could go to friends of his, constantly changing his hiding place. We waited two or three days more because we couldn't comprehend that such a calamitous thing could happen, but we finally put our plan into action. I would come back secretly at intervals, but even then I was in a hurry to leave. We sent Alionushka to stay with Lev's sister-in-law.

*The "Liebestraum" by Liszt, played by one of the people
who took refuge in the Krupinskys' apartment*

"Liebestraum" (List.)

Mysterious agitations started at about that time. At night, from the Krupinskys' apartment we could hear shouting and shots from the street. Who was firing on whom? We hid under our bedcovers when the shooting started, then went to look out the window from which we could see the German camp. One night rockets were fired in the air, and we realized it was the Germans' New Year! The *niania* of the Krupinsky children said, "They will go and it will be a great calamity for us."

In the evening we often sat in the dining room, the windows of which gave onto a courtyard. Ellochka and her husband George, one as charming as the other, did their best to alleviate the sadness of our existence. Fortunately they also had staying with them a man, either a guest or someone in hiding, who was an excellent pianist, and most evenings, as none of us felt like going to bed, we listened to him or to George playing Chopin or Liszt, particularly Liszt's "Liebestraum", which we asked him to play again and again. The sublimity of "Liebestraum" somehow made the reality of our situation disappear in a sad mist.

N OW THE GERMANS were moving out again, and we knew that anarchy would return. When I insisted that we flee to Odessa before the Germans left, Lev agreed, because living in hiding was extremely hard on him. Early in the morning of the day after Christmas, we left by train, feeling nervous and sad and expecting to be arrested any minute.

Our life in Odessa from the end of December to May 1919 was grey and dull. The French were in control of Odessa when we arrived, but we soon heard rumours that they too were planning to leave. That decided us to go to Constantinople. Lev started making the necessary arrangements with the French authorities, which wasn't easy and took a long time. We were finally given our passports and bought tickets on the first ship to leave Odessa, the *Alexander III*. We went aboard that very evening. It was not until the following evening that we departed; it was still light as I stood on deck and watched Russia recede. I felt calmer and a strange weight lifted from me. When there was no longer any sight of land I crossed myself. Goodbye Russia!

Deeds of years gone by,
a legend from the distant past
(Pushkin)

DAVYDOFF FAMILY TREE

The names of people who appear in the book are printed here in **bold type**.

R. K. Feleizen
= Marya Vassilyevna
1819–45

Mikhail Vassilyevich
1820–80

Ekaterina Vassilyevna
"Aunt Katya"
1821–98
=
Vassily Peresleny

Elisaveta Vassilyevna
"Aunt Lisa"
1823–1902

Pyotr Vassilyevich
1825–1912
=
Elisaveta Sergeyevna
b. Princess Trubetzkoy
1834–1918

Olga Alexandrovna
b. Princess Lieven
1857–1923
=
Vassily Petrovich
1852–1900

Olga Iakovlevna
b. de Miller
1899–1975
=
Alexander Vassilyevich
"Sasha"
1881–1955

Pyotr Vassilyevich
"Petya"
1879–1916

Vassily Vassilyevich
"Vassya"
1877–?

J. M. Dax
=
Olga Alexandrovna
1928–

Manya Nikolaevna

Varvara Nikolaevna

Nina Nikolaevna

Kolya Sandberg

Verochka Sandberg

Natasha Dikov

Shura Pissarev

Katya Pissarev

Nikolai Vassilyevich
"Uncle Nicholas"
1826–1916

Vassily Vassilyevich
1829–73

Vassily Lvovich
Davydoff
"Decembrist"
1792–1854
=
Alexandra Ivanovna
b. Potapova
1802–94

Alexandra Vassilyevna

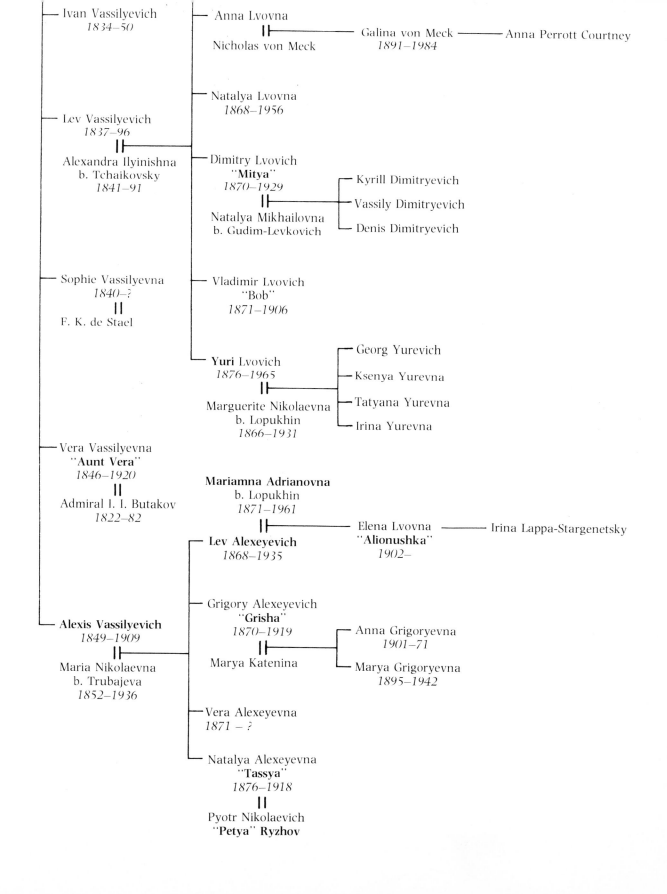

Ivan Vassilyevich
1834–50

Anna Lvovna
Nicholas von Meck

Galina von Meck ——— Anna Perrott Courtney
1891–1984

Natalya Lvovna
1868–1956

Lev Vassilyevich
1837–96

Alexandra Ilyinishna
b. Tchaikovsky
1841–91

Dimitry Lvovich
"Mitya"
1870–1929

Natalya Mikhailovna
b. Gudim-Levkovich

Kyrill Dimitryevich

Vassily Dimitryevich

Denis Dimitryevich

Sophie Vassilyevna
1840–?

F. K. de Stael

Vladimir Lvovich
"Bob"
1871–1906

Yuri Lvovich
1876–1965

Marguerite Nikolaevna
b. Lopukhin
1866–1931

Georg Yurevich

Ksenya Yurevna

Tatyana Yurevna

Irina Yurevna

Vera Vassilyevna
"Aunt Vera"
1846–1920

Admiral I. I. Butakov
1822–82

Mariamna Adrianovna
b. Lopukhin
1871–1961

Lev Alexeyevich
1868–1935

Elena Lvovna
"Alionushka"
1902–

Irina Lappa-Stargenetsky

Grigory Alexeyevich
"Grisha"
1870–1919

Marya Katenina

Anna Grigoryevna
1901–71

Marya Grigoryevna
1895–1942

Alexis Vassilyevich
1849–1909

Maria Nikolaevna
b. Trubajeva
1852–1936

Vera Alexeyevna
1871 – ?

Natalya Alexeyevna
"Tassya"
1876–1918

Pyotr Nikolaevich
"Petya" Ryzhov